Millennarian Views:

WITH

REASONS FOR RECEIVING THEM.

TO WHICH IS ADDED A DISCOURSE ON

The Fact and Nature of the Resurrection.

BY

ALFRED BRYANT,
PASTOR OF THE FIRST PRESBYTERIAN CHURCH, NILES, MICHIGAN.

NEW YORK:
PUBLISHED BY M. W. DODD,
Brick Church Chapel, City Hall Square, opposite the City Hall

1852.

E. O. Jenkins, Printer,
114 Nassau Street.

PREFACE.

It was the intention to issue the following treatise without offering any apology, or assigning any reasons for its publication; but the counsel of others have induced a brief statement.

Among the reasons which have prompted the present work are, first: A desire to give publicity to views which are conscientiously believed to be a part, and a very important part of the gospel of our Lord and Saviour Jesus Christ. The fact that others differ from us in this conviction, and believe that no good can result from the spread of these views, cannot alter our own long-pondered, and long-cherished persuasion; any more than the fact that many differ with us in respect to the importance of the doctrines of grace, can diminish our solemn conviction of their essential character. Another reason for the appearance of the present work, is the inquiry often made within the circle of the author's acquaintance and influence, what is millennarianism? Not knowing of any single work which was adapted to give a clear and connected view of the whole subject, to those who have not the time or means to read and investigate extensively, the author has undertaken, in compliance with the wishes of his own people especially, to answer the question as he believes it is generally held. The work, therefore, is not designed to be critical, but mostly biblical—answering the title assumed, Millennarian Views with Reasons derived from the Scriptures for receiving them.

But these considerations might never have given birth to this work, had it not been for the repeated misrepresentations made through the press and other channels. We do not accuse our brethren of any thing intentionally unjust or unkind. No doubt they have stated what they supposed to be the truth, but their misapprehensions, and misstatements are none the less painful on this account, or injurious to our standing and influence. We have so often been placed in a false and painful position, and so many suspicions have been excited, that we have been compelled to write in defence of the truth, and ourselves.

Can we be expected to remain silent, when what we hold as sacred and precious, is misrepresented and ridiculed? If we are in error we desire to be convinced; but then, those who would effectually convince us of our sin, must first be sure that they understand our views—must view and state them as we do, and then must kindly and charitably meet our arguments as presented. It is the hope of the author, that truth and charity may result from these pages.

ONTENTS.

CHAPTER EIGHTH.

CHAPTER NINTH.

MILLENNARIAN VIEWS,

WITH

REASONS FOR RECEIVING THEM.

Chapter First.

INTRODUCTION.

Kind Reader:—Your attention is invited to a subject deeply interesting and important. It is not the design of this book to assail you as an antagonist, or to overturn the foundation of apostles and prophets, Jesus Christ himself being the chief corner-stone.

Though the views which will be advocated are deemed exceedingly important and comforting, yet they are not to be exalted above those essential doctrines held by the Christian church, around which the believer's hopes of immortal glory cluster. Were the writer called upon to state, in the order of importance, his own convictions of the truths of revelation, first, and above all, would be named Jesus Christ, God manifest in the flesh, and the atonement he made when he bore our sins in his own body on the tree. Around the cross as their centre and source, would be placed the influences of the spirit, the doctrines of justification by faith, regeneration, repentance, sanctification, and the necessity of good works, as the fruit and evidence of a renewed and justified state.

But in connection with all these, as the glory to which they point, and to which they were designed to elevate the redeemed, would be enumerated God's exceeding great and precious promises of future reward, and all his revealed purposes of grace respecting the ransomed church on earth, and through eternal ages.

For what did Jesus suffer and die, but to redeem unto himself a peculiar people zealous of good works, and to raise them to a participation with himself, in all the glories of his eternal kingdom? The promises which assure the believer of all this, and the prophecies which unfold the nature, extent, and blessedness of the kingdom of God, as objects of faith and motives to obedience, cannot be unessential to the great scheme of redeeming mercy, or neglected without injuring its fair proportions.

Now, should any, from right apprehension, and from intelligent and conscientious conviction, dissent from the views to be presented, in regard to the import of those promises and prophecies, which unfold the future purposes of God respecting his own dear church and the world, it is hoped that true believers will not disagree in regard to those great and fundamental truths already named, which range themselves around the cross of Christ, as the ground-work of every good hope through grace.

These are indeed not vain things; they are our life. They are the corner stones—the foundation, which, if removed, the superstructure must fall, however imposing, with all its top-stones of ornament and beauty.

If in the cross and its associated doctrines there is agreement, and all are truly united to Christ by a living and a life-giving faith, we are fellow-heirs of the kingdom prepared from the foundation of the world, though some are mistaken in regard to its nature and manifold results.

It is, indeed, a delightful and soul-cheering truth, amid the errors and imperfection of the present world, that all who are built upon the foundation of apostles and prophets, Jesus Christ himself being the chief corner-stone, are safe, however widely they may differ in the externals of religion, or in the import of those promises which leave untouched the essential truths of the gospel.

Other foundation can no man lay than that which is laid, which is Jesus Christ. Now if any man build upon this foundation, gold, silver, precious stones, wood, hay, stubble, every man's work shall be made manifest: for the day shall declare it, because it shall be revealed by fire; and the fire shall try every man's work, of what sort it is. If any man's work abide which he hath built thereupon, he shall receive a reward. If any man's work shall be burned, he shall suffer loss: but he himself shall be saved; yet so as by fire. 1 Cor.

And what immense loss many may suffer, though saved, from the errors they may have imbibed and taught.

How anxious should every one be, then, to know all that God has revealed, and to have all his views conformed harmoniously and consistently to all that the prophets have foretold. How can any portion of the word of God be neglected with impunity? or how can any say, that this or that portion of revealed truth may be passed by or innocently remain unstudied? For he that shall break one of the least of these my commandments, and shall teach men so, he shall be called the least in the kingdom of God. These are solemn considerations, and they admonish all to circumspection, and earnest study and prayer.

No infallibility will be set up in these pages; but yet, conscious of infirmity, and prone to err, we desire with kindness and earnestness to advocate views, which in all charity to those who may differ, we sincerely and solemnly believe to be the truth of God.

In attempting to establish the positions which may be

taken, no resort will be made to any new or strange principles of interpretation. No others are desired, than those uniformly adopted by all evangelical Christians, in proving the supreme divinity of our Lord, the doctrines of the atonement, justification, regeneration, the resurrection of the dead, and a day of judgment, when we must all appear before the judgment seat of Christ to receive according to the deeds done in the body. To all these and kindred doctrines, a hearty assent is given; because they are clearly revealed in scripture, and any interpretation of any portion of the word of God which would set them aside must be erroneous.

By the same mode of interpretation, by which the existence of a heaven and a hell, and an endless duration of happiness and misery are proved from scripture, the second glorious appearing of our Lord Jesus Christ to judge the quick and the dead, and all those events which are associated with his coming, will be proved.

That the views advocated, and the terms used, may be clearly understood, especially by those who may be unacquainted with the subject, it will be necessary to make some explanations.

The term Millennium, means a thousand years. It is commonly employed to denote that glorious period predicted in many scriptures, when all this world shall be converted to Christ, and all, from the least unto the greatest, be brought to know and serve the Lord.

The idea of a millennium, or a thousand years of glorious prosperity to the church of God on earth, freed from the influences of the wicked one, is taken from Rev. 20, 1–7.

"And I saw an angel come down from heaven, having the key of the bottomless pit and a great chain in his hand. And he laid hold on the dragon, that old serpent, which is the devil and satan, and bound him a thousand years, and cast him into the bottomless pit, and shut him up, and set a seal upon him, that he should deceive the nations no more, till the thousand years should be fulfilled; and after this, he must be loosed a little season.

And I saw thrones, and they sat upon them, and judgment was given unto them: and I saw the souls of them that were beheaded for the witness of Jesus, and for the word of God, and which had not worshipped the beast, neither his image, neither had received his mark upon their foreheads, or in their hands; and they lived and reigned with Christ a thousand years. But the rest of the dead lived not again until the thousand years were finished. This is the first resurrection.

"Blessed and holy is he that hath part in the first resurrection: on such the second death hath no power, but they shall be priests of God and of Christ, and shall reign with him a thousand years."

This passage is generally understood to denote a period of triumph and exalted prosperity of the Church on earth, such as never before has been experienced; and the binding of Satan, and his dejection to the pit, to represent his exclusion from the world.

Now, all who believe in the prosperity of the Church on earth for a thousand years, are in fact millennarians, whatever may be their views of the nature of the kingdom which Jesus Christ is to exercise over the world.

But the term millennarian, is now generally employed to designate those who believe in the pre-millennial advent of Christ, and his personal reign on earth with his saints, with associated doctrines. In this sense the term will be employed in the following discourses, while the term spiritualist, will represent those who believe only in a spiritual reign. The writer does not profess to be the authorized expounder of Millennarianism; but it is believed, that in all the great leading doctrines and reasonings here presented, there is an entire agreement with what others have written, and pre-millennialists uniformly hold. He is not aware that there is a single new view presented in the book.

In the manner of illustration, every man must have his own way, and in the discussion of details not clearly revealed, there must and will be differences in opinion here, as on every other subject. But if there is not entire agreement among millennarians, widely separated, and differently constituted and educated, can this be urged as a legitimate argument against their views? What doctrine and truth of the Christian religion might not be repudiated and rejected on this ground? Unbelievers assign often, as a reason for rejecting the Bible, that Christians are so much disagreed among themselves as to what it teaches. Is such an argument fair or safe? And shall Christians refuse candidly to examine the arguments of millennarians, because there is not perfect unanimity among themselves on all points? There are some very conflicting opinions among Christians in regard to the nature of the atonement, and kindred doctrines. Shall we give them up, and say there is no certain truth in the atonement, nothing definite here upon which the sin-burdened soul can rest—no real fountain opened for sin and uncleanness, because men in their presumption, or weakness, or ignorance, go beyond the bounds of revelation, and form conflicting theories? Surely not.

> "For me, when I forget the darling theme,
> Be my tongue mute, my fancy paint no more,
> And, dead to joy, forget this heart to beat."

But the differences in opinion in regard to the millennium or the conversion of the world, which are used as convertible terms, are not mostly on the side of millennarians.

Professor Stuart maintains, in his work on the Apocalypse, that many heathen nations, without the limits of the Roman empire, will remain unevangelized during all the long years of the millennium, and these will be the nations which Satan will go out to deceive after he is loosed from his prison.

Dr. Buchanan, in his Asiatic Researches, holds that this world never is to be converted in fact; but that the description of our Lord in the 24th chapter of Matthew, of wars, and rumors of wars, of troubles, and revolutions, are absolutely to continue up to the end of the world.

While Mr. Harris, in his "Great Commission," insists that the world will be so thoroughly converted, that heaven will dawn on earth.

Many pages might be filled with a recital of the widely conflicting views of those who are professedly united in their efforts for a world's conversion. Let any one take the trouble to make definite inquiries among public speakers and teachers upon this subject, and he will be surprised to learn how exceedingly indefinite and contradictory are the opinions of many. Brethren beloved have frequently acknowledged that this is a subject to which they have never given any attention, and upon which they have formed no estimate. Shall those, therefore, who differ so widely among themselves, reject millennarian views, because those who hold them are not perfectly agreed upon every point of detail? Upon this principle, and for the same reason, we might be justified in rejecting the idea of the conversion of the world altogether, and in denying all obligation to labor for it.

But who shall decide amid this "war of elements," the "conclusions retrograde, and mad mistake" which many draw? God in his word. Our appeal must be to the law and the testimony. These are the only infallible rules of faith and practice. Here we are one. And now if it is the will of God that we should pray for the coming of his kingdom, and live and labor in view of this promised kingdom, he has certainly revealed to us something definite and certain respecting it; for is it reasonable to suppose that he would require us to pray for what was not revealed, or to labor for what was so obscurely and uncertainly promised, that even by searching we could not arrive at any certain conclusion as to what was meant? It seems to us that the scriptures are as definite and clear upon this subject of the coming kingdom, as upon any other within the range of revelation. God has certainly revealed a great and wide-circling scheme of mercy in his word, embodied in the prophecies, which cannot be neglected with impunity. It will be the design of the following pages to unfold this scheme as we understand it, and leave each one to decide "what is truth," according to the scriptures.

Chapter Second.

IN WHAT SENSE DO THE SCRIPTURES TEACH THAT THE WORLD WILL BE CONVERTED? AND WHEN?

THE conversion of the world, in some manner and form, is manifestly the great idea of the age. In all the great benevolent enterprises of the present day, in all efforts for the amelioration of the condition of suffering humanity, and in all the rapid and onward progress of knowledge and science, there is no one thing among Christians, about which more is heard or said, than the conversion or evangelization of all the nations and families of the earth. It is presented as the great motive to action, the bright vision which gilds the future, the consummation of earthly bliss, and is made the solace of the church in all her conflicts with error and sin.

Now, it is not denied by millennarians, that the world will be at some future time all converted, and converted too in a far higher and more glorious sense, than is commonly held by those who oppose their views.

Human speculations and theories upon a subject of this nature are vain and injurious. The future can only be known and revealed by Him, who sees the end from the beginning. To His teachings, then, it should be the desire of all to yield, believingly and obediently. Let us turn to the law and the testimony, and hear what saith the Lord.

The apostle John assures us, that "For this purpose was

the Son of God manifested, that he might destroy the works of the devil." 1 John. 3 : 8.

This statement is very explicit and clear in setting forth the great design of the Saviour's mission.

But what are the works of the devil, which our Lord came to destroy? Undoubtedly, all that in the world which is the fruit of his first and subsequent temptations. Sin in all its forms, is the work of the devil; for, "He that committeth sin, is of the devil; for the devil sinneth from the beginning. He is a liar, and the father of lies." And not only sin, but death the consequence and curse of sin; "for by one man sin entered into the world, and death by sin, and so death has passed upon all men, for that all have sinned." And hence we are told, 2 Tim. 1 : 10, that Jesus Christ was manifested, to abolish death, and to bring life and immortality to light through the gospel.

It is clearly predicted in these passages, that the great Redeemer, in the consummation of His work of salvation on earth, will annul the curse of death, and wipe clean out, the mementos of the grave.

The curse of barrenness under which the earth groans, and the woes which have come in varied forms upon creation, animate and inanimate, for man's revolt, are the works of the devil.

And if the Son of God was manifested to destroy the works of the devil, and He finishes and perfects his work in righteousness, then the time is coming when all sin, and all its fruits and woful consequences, will be banished from our world, and earth restored to its Eden purity and glory.

In Acts 3 : 19–21, a time of the restitution of all things is spoken of, which very clearly illustrates and confirms the views above stated.

"Repent ye, therefore, and be converted, that your sins may be blotted out, when the times of refreshing shall come from the presence of the Lord; and he shall send Jesus Christ, which before was preached unto you: Whom the heavens must receive, until the times of the restitution of all things, which God hath spoken by the mouth of all His holy prophets since the world began."

But what is meant by the restitution of all things, here predicted?

The term restitution, αποκαταστασις, Bloomfield says, "properly signifies a restoration of anything to some former state," and by implication for the better. Robinson, in his Greek lexicon, gives the same definition, and refers its use "to Messiah's future reign or kingdom." Webster, in his quarto Dictionary, defines the word restitution to mean, among other things, "The act of recovering a former state, or posture;" and then referring to this passage in Acts, he says, "Restitution of all things, is, the putting the world in a holy and happy state."

This is undoubtedly the meaning of the term, and hence it cannot refer, as some teach, to the exaltation of the righteous to heaven, or the consummation of all things at the last day, as commonly understood, for there is no restoration in any of these things, in the sense described, to a former and better state previously possessed. It could not be said of the Jews that they would be restored to their own land, if they had never before dwelt in it, nor of any man that he was restored to an office which he never before held.

Now, if this restitution of all things is spoken of by all God's holy prophets since the world began, then certainly, without any doubt or speculation, we can, by searching the scriptures, learn what the apostle means.

But before this is done, let us notice another remarkable passage in Matt. 19: 27, 28, in which the same great and glorious truth respecting the restitution of all things is revealed.

"Then answered Peter, and said unto him, behold, we have forsaken all, and followed thee; what shall we have therefore? And Jesus said unto them, Verily I say unto you, that ye which have followed me, in the regeneration when the Son of man shall sit in the throne of his glory, ye also shall sit upon the twelve thrones, judging the twelve tribes of Israel."

There is then, according to the teaching of our Lord, to be a time of regeneration, specially and emphatically so denominated. The term, regeneration, means reproduction, the act of forming into a new and better state. Robinson, in his Greek Lexicon, says of the original word, "That it refers to the complete external manifestation of Messiah's kingdom, when all things are to be delivered from their present corruption and restored to spiritual purity and splendor."

Now this complete and perfect restoration and regeneration of all things, brought to view in these interesting passages, are predicted clearly, and somewhat in detail by the holy prophets.

1. Man's entire restoration to holiness and happiness is predicted.

To save time and room, we shall not stop to inquire, at present, whether the passages quoted refer to Jews or Gentiles, as the design is to prove that all men of whatever nation are to be restored.

Isaiah 2: 2–5. "And it shall come to pass in the last days, that the mountain of the Lord's house shall be established in the top of the mountains, and shall be exalted above the hills; and all nations shall flow unto it. And many people shall go, and say, come ye, and let us go up to the mountain of the Lord, to the house of the God of Jacob; and he will teach us of his ways, and we will walk in his paths; for out of Zion shall go forth the law, and the word of the Lord from Jerusalem. And he shall judge among the nations, and shall rebuke many people: and they shall beat their swords into plough-shares, and their spears into pruning-hooks: nation shall not lift up sword against nation, neither shall they learn war any more."

Is. 11 : 9. "They shall not hurt nor destroy in all my holy mountains: for the earth shall be full of the knowledge of the Lord, as the waters cover the sea."

Jeremiah 31: 34. "But this shall be the covenant that I will make with the house of Israel; after those days, saith the Lord, I will put my law in their inward parts, and write it in their hearts; and will be their God, and they shall be my people. And they shall teach no more every man his neighbor, and every man his brother, saying, know the Lord: for they shall all know me from the least of them unto the greatest of them, saith the Lord."

Isaiah 52: 10. "The Lord hath made bare his holy arm in the eyes of all the nations: and all the ends of the earth shall see the salvation of our God."

Isaiah 60: 18–21. "Violence shall no more be heard in thy land, wasting nor destruction within thy borders; but thou shalt call thy walls salvation, and thy gates praise. The sun shall be no more thy light by day: neither for brightness shall the moon give light unto thee: but the Lord shall be unto thee an everlasting light, and thy God thy glory.

"Thy sun shall no more go down; neither shall thy moon withdraw itself: for the Lord shall be thine everlasting light, and the days of thy mourning shall be ended. Thy people also shall be all righteous: they shall inherit the land forever, the branch of my planting, the work of my hands, that I may be glorified. A little one shall become a thousand, and a small one a strong nation: I the Lord will hasten it in its time."

Surely universal holiness, universal happiness, and uninterrupted and eternal prosperity, could not be more strongly and beautifully foretold, than they are in this sublime passage, which manifestly has a special reference to the Jewish nation.

Isaiah 45: 22, 23. "Look unto me and be ye saved, all ye ends of the earth: for I am God and there is none else. I have sworn by myself, the word is gone out of my mouth in righteousness, and shall not return, that unto me every knee shall bow and every tongue shall swear."

These words teach that the time will come when every person on earth shall consecrate himself to God, to love and obey him forever.

Psalms 12: 17. "Yea, all kings shall fall down before him, all nations shall serve him." 5: 17. "His name shall endure forever, his name shall be continued as long as the sun, and men shall be blessed in him; all nations shall call him blessed." 86: 9. "All nations whom thou hast made shall come and worship before thee, O Lord, and shall glorify thy name."

Malachi 1: 11. "For from the rising of the sun even unto the going down of the same, my name shall be great among the Gentiles; and in every place incense shall be offered unto my name, and a pure offering: for my name shall be great among the heathen saith the Lord of hosts."

Isaiah 65: 17–19. "For behold, I create new heavens and a new earth: and the former shall not be remembered, nor come into mind." "But be ye glad and rejoice forever in that which I create: for behold, I create Jerusalem a rejoicing and her people a joy. And I will rejoice in Jerusalem, and joy in my people: and the voice of weeping shall no more be heard in her, nor the voice of crying."

Daniel 7: 27. "And the kingdom and dominion, and the greatness of the kingdom under the whole heaven, shall be given to the people of the saints of the Most High, whose kingdom is an everlasting kingdom, and all dominions shall serve and obey him."

Other scriptures might be quoted to the same point, but if these do not teach that all men, universally and individually, are yet to be regenerated and restored to holiness and happiness, then to us there is no certain meaning in language. And all that is here predicted is just that for which we are taught to pray by our Lord.

"Thy kingdom come. Thy will be done on earth as it is in heaven." How many offer this prayer without considering, or believing its full and glorious import. Our Lord would certainly never teach us to pray for what he knew would never be granted, or for what he never intended to accomplish. But if it is ever fully answered, and it must be, as God is faithful and true, then the time is coming, most assuredly, when the will of God will be done on earth as it is in heaven, by every individual, perfectly, joyfully, universally. This petition, therefore, may be regarded as a revelation of the will of God concerning our world, and a pledge that all which holy men, inspired by the Holy Ghost, have written, will be fulfilled. And all this is in perfect harmony with the revealed purpose of the Son of God, to destroy *in our world* the works of the devil.

And when these things come to pass, then will be fulfilled another most interesting and significant saying of the Saviour: "And I, if I be lifted up from the earth will draw all men unto me;" yes, all men, not simply some of all classes and nations; but all, universally, from the least unto the greatest of them. This declaration of our Lord is clearly prophetic of what will be the grand result and consummation of his atonement, in a redeemed and regenerated world. Thus it may be seen, that the glowing descriptions of Old Testament prophets respecting the restoration of our world from sin, are responded to by all the annunciations of the New. But—

2. Not only is man's restoration to holiness and happiness predicted; but it is also foretold, by the holy prophets, that sickness and death, the curse and consequence of sin, shall at some future period be no more.

And why should they not be removed? Can they hold sway in a world redeemed and purified from sin?

If sin is removed, why not all its fruits and curse? And if the Son of God was manifested to destroy the works of the Devil, must he not destroy these as well as sin?

Isaiah 33: 22–24. "For the Lord is our Judge; the Lord is our Lawgiver, the Lord is our King; he will save us. *And the inhabitants shall not say I am sick;* the people that dwell there shall be forgiven their iniquity."

The absence of all sickness, and causes of pain or sorrow, is implied in all those prophetic promises, already recited, which declare that the voice of weeping and sorrow shall be known no more. This could never be true in regard to any people, were sickness, and pain, and death to exist as they do now.

Isaiah 25: 6–8. "And in this mountain shall the Lord of hosts make unto all people a feast of fat things, a feast of wines on the lees, of fat things full of marrow, of wines on the lees well refined. And he will destroy in this mountain the face of the covering cast over all people, and the veil that is spread over all nations. *He will swallow up death in victory,* and the Lord God will wipe away tears from off all faces, and the rebuke of his people shall he take away from off all the earth, for the Lord hath spoken it.

This passage most clearly predicts a victory over death and the grave at the time here indicated, when the Lord God will wipe away tears from off all faces, and take away all chastisements and punishments from earth. And let it be noticed, that this is a description of a state of things, not in that glorious abode of God we call heaven, but its designation is here upon the earth.

The same thing is foretold in Rev. 21 : 2–4, which describes a state of things among men in this world.

"And I John saw the holy city, new Jerusalem, *coming down from God out of heaven*, prepared as a bride adorned for her husband.

"And I heard a great voice out of heaven, saying, Behold, the tabernacle of God is with men, and he will dwell with them, and they shall be his people, and God himself shall be with them, and be their God.

"And God shall wipe away all tears from their eyes; and there shall be no more death, neither sorrow, nor crying, neither shall there be any more pain: for the former things are passed away. And he that sat upon the throne said, Behold, I make all things new. And he said unto me, Write; for these words are true and faithful."

How solemnly and emphatically does the Lord here assure us, that he will yet create all things new in our world, so that the former state of sin, suffering, and death, shall be no more. And when all this is accomplished, and not till then, will the Son of God have completely destroyed on earth the works of the devil. But—

3. When man fell the ground was cursed for his sake; "Thorns and thistles shall it bring forth, and of the sweat of thy face shalt thou eat bread, until thou return to the ground from which thou wast taken."

Now, it is predicted that this curse shall be removed; and why must it not be as a curse of sin, and a part of the work of the devil?

Isa. 55 : 12, 13. "For ye shall go out with joy, and be led forth with peace; the mountains and hills shall break forth before you into singing, and all the trees of the field shall clap their hands. Instead of the thorn shall come up the fir-tree, and instead of the briar shall come up the myrtle tree; and it shall be to the Lord for a name, for an everlasting sign that shall not be cut off."

In this passage, the very curse pronounced upon the ground for man's sin, is named to be removed; and in bold personification, the exuberant fertility of earth is joyously foretold.

Isa. 41: 18–20. "I will open rivers in high places, and fountains in the midst of the valleys; I will make the wilderness a pool of water, and dry land springs of water. I will plant in the wilderness the cedar, the shittah tree, and the myrtle, and the oil tree; I will set in the desert the fir tree, and the pine, and the box tree, together: That they may see, and know, and consider, and understand together, that the hand of the Lord hath done this, and the Holy One of Israel hath created it."

Nothing like this has ever yet occurred on earth, and it must consequently be future.

The language is beautifully descriptive of the restoration of our world to its primitive beauty and fertility, when all the curse that has come upon it, as a chastisement of sinful man, shall be annulled by the power of God, as one of the fruits of the Saviour's purchase.

Is. 35: 1–10. At the time that "the ransomed of the Lord shall return, and come to Zion with songs and everlasting joy upon their heads; and when they shall obtain joy and gladness, and sorrow and sighing shall flee away;" we are told—

"The wilderness and solitary places shall be glad for them; and the desert shall rejoice and blossom as the rose. It shall blossom abundantly, and rejoice, even with joy and singing; the glory of Lebanon shall be given unto it, the excellency of Carmel, and Sharon, they shall see the glory of the Lord, and the excellency of our God.

"Then the eyes of the blind shall be opened, and the ears of the deaf shall be unstopped. Then shall the lame man leap as a hart, and the tongue of the dumb sing: for in the wilderness shall waters break out, and streams in the desert.

"And the parched ground shall become a pool, and the thirsty land springs of water; in the habitation of dragons, where each lay, shall be grass with reeds and rushes."

The whole chapter from which this is taken, is a most beautiful and joyous description of the fertility, and prosperity, and happy state of our world under the future reign of Messiah, when there shall be such geological changes and transformations effected that the desert wastes of Arabia and Africa, and all the world, shall become fruitful as the garden of God, and yield their joyful abundance for the teeming and happy millions of earth.

And there is nothing impossible, or absurd, in receiving this description as true, in its most natural and obvious import. Why should it not be so? Must our world forever remain under the curse, even when sin and death are removed? Will it be beneath the love and dignity and power of God, to accomplish even this, in the glorious consummation of his salvation to our world?

If Heaven so ordains, all this may be effected without a miracle, by the natural operation of those laws and agencies which are now at work upon, within, and through the earth. And back of all these, reposes his infinite power, which he can exert at any moment, if need be, miraculously, to accomplish his word, and this we believe he will do. Why, then, should we doubt, or hesitate to receive the word of God in its simple, full, and joyous import? But—

4. It is also predicted that in this restored world, redeemed from sin and the curse, the ferocity of animals shall be subdued, and their subjugation to man, in all things, fully

accomplished, as we may suppose they would have been, had sin never entered Eden.

Isaiah 11 : 1–9. "And there shall come forth a rod out of the stem of Jesse, and a branch shall grow out of his roots: and the spirit of the Lord shall rest upon him, the spirit of wisdom and understanding, the spirit of counsel and might, the spirit of knowledge and the fear of the Lord. And he shall make him of quick understanding in the fear of the Lord: and he shall not judge after the sight of his eyes, neither reprove after the hearing of his ear: but with righteousness shall he judge the poor, and reprove with equity for the meek of the earth: and he shall smite the earth with the rod of his mouth, and with the breath of his lips shall he slay the wicked. And righteousness shall be the girdle of his loins, and faithfulness the girdle of his reins. The wolf also shall dwell with the lamb, and the leopard shall lie down with the kid; and the calf and the young lion, and the fatling together; and a little child shall lead them. And the cow and the bear shall feed; their young ones shall lie down together: and the lion shall eat straw like the ox. And the sucking child shall play on the hole of the asp, and the weaned child shall put his hand in the cockatrice's den. They shall not hurt or destroy in all my holy mountain: for the earth shall be full of the knowledge of the Lord, as the waters cover the sea."

The same prediction in regard to the docility of these animals may be found in Isaiah 65: 25.

Thus it is definitely foretold, that during the peaceful and happy reign of the Son of David—the Messiah, on earth, the ferocity of animals shall be subdued, and that in respect to man they shall be entirely harmless and subservient.

The full meaning of these predictions, I suppose to be, that in this restored and glorious era, during the reign of Christ on earth, these animals will be entirely domesticated, as is now the cat, and the dog, and be at peace among themselves, under the guidance and subduing power of God and man.

And all that is here predicted may be accomplished by divine influence, without supposing any miraculous change in their natures. Let us suppose that all the deserts, and wildernesses, and solitary places, shall be inhabited and cultivated as predicted, then there would be no place for these animals, except as they existed in tameness and domestication.

The facts here stated, that these animals shall feed together, and that the lion shall eat straw like the ox, that is, shall share in such vegetable food as may be provided for them by man, are not absurd or impossible. The word straw, here, undoubtedly stands for all kinds of vegetable food. We know that the bear now feeds on this, and we have seen the cat and the dog eat vegetable food frequently, and why may not the leopard and lion, when brought into a state of domestication? And the facts stated in the prophecy do not declare that they may not also eat animal food when given to them. When it is said, "They shall not hurt or destroy in all my holy mountain," it means that they shall be docile and harmless in respect to man. There would be no violation of the prediction, should these animals named eat such animal food as might be provided and appropriated for them.

And all this, in the judgment of the writer, would be perfectly consistent with a world redeemed from sin and the curse.

It is, we think, a mistaken idea of many, that death among animals, and all inferior creatures, is in consequence of the sin of man. This is altogether an assumption, for which there is no scriptural proof. Though Adam was the representative head of his race, and as such introduced sin and death among them, it is never said that he stood as the representative of animals, birds, and insects, and introduced death among them.

Can any one rationally suppose that no animal, insect, or animalcula would ever have died, had not man sinned? Is the fact that many of the fish of river, sea and ocean, are formed to live on, and devour each other by millions daily, a curse for man's revolt?

Would no bird ever have picked up a worm or a bug, had not man sinned? Would no one animalcula, which live and revel in every drop of water, and upon every vegetable, have been consumed by man or beast in the water they drink or the food they eat? And yet the destruction of the smallest insect involves the same principle of life as does the destruction of an ox.

By the microscope, one animalcula is seen greedily to devour another. Is this a curse for the sin of man?

The fact is, the anatomical and physiological formation of all carniverous animals, shows that they were designed, by the Creator, to live on just such food as is provided for them, and as their wisely adapted powers enable them to procure. And hence it is said, "The young lions roar after their prey, and seek their meat from God, and that which he gives them they gather." And so he provides for man and beast.

The peculiar contrivance and adaptation in each animal to the food it is to eat, and all the powers given to secure it, furnish the most conclusive evidence of the existence and providence of an all-wise, and benevolent Creator. And are all these contrivances and adaptations, showing the wisdom and handy work of God, the result of sin in man?

Surely no one is authorized to believe any such thing, unless it is so revealed by God. But it is not.

When it is said by the apostle, that "By one man sin entered into the world, and death by sin," he only speaks in reference to man, and so immediately explains himself;

"And so death has passed upon all men, for that all have sinned."

It is not here said that death passed upon animals because man sinned. They were never designed to be immortal. Were there no destruction among them by each other, death would no doubt come upon them by a necessary law of organized matter, of decay and reproduction.

When God said to our first parents, "In the day thou eatest thereof, thou shalt surely die," it is clearly implied, that should they not sin they would not die. There would have been no meaning in the penalty denounced were it not true, that they would have been preserved to immortality, had their innocence been maintained.

But why would not man have died in innocence? was not his animal nature subject to the same laws as others? Is there any proof in scripture that he was immortal in his physical nature, independently of means and appropriate agencies to sustain it? Not any.

The fact that food was provided for him, and that it was necessary for him to eat in innocence, shows that he might have wasted away and perished had he not eaten.

Why then would he not have died, had he not sinned? Simply because God had provided an antidote in Eden—the means of sustaining him in immortal youth and vigor: for thus it is written, "And out of the ground made the Lord God to grow every tree that is pleasant to the sight and good for food; the tree of life also in the midst of the garden."

What then was the design of this tree of life, or this life-bearing tree? Evidently to perpetuate life—to preserve youth and vigor; by partaking of its fruit. And there is nothing unreasonable or absurd in this. God, in his providence, gives to ordinary food the power of sustaining life for a limited time. Why might he not, then, if he chose, give to some particular fruit the property of sustaining man's physical nature to immortality? This was the nature of the tree of life. It had the same power to preserve the functions of life in all their integrity for unlimited duration that ordinary food has to repair the wastes of each day. Its properties were such as would answer the purposes of its creation, in counteracting the tendencies of time to impair and destroy man's physical energies.

Hence the method adopted of enforcing the sentence of death.

"And the Lord God said, Behold, the man is become as one of us, to know good and evil: and now, lest he put forth his hand, and take also of the tree of life, and eat, and live forever: Therefore the Lord God sent him forth from the garden of Eden, to till the ground from whence he was taken. So he drove out the man: and he placed at the east of the garden of Eden, Cherubim, and a flaming sword which turned every way, to keep the way of the tree of life."

It is clear from this, that man would have continued to have lived on to immortality, notwithstanding his sin, had he been permitted to eat of the tree of life, which clearly indicates the nature and properties and design of the tree.

And hence, from the moment he was debarred access to the tree of life, he was condemned to death, in common with the animal world around him. Partaking of the tree of knowledge of good and evil, in violation of command, worked a forfeiture of the tree of life, and the laws of nature, in due time, effectually worked out the penalty.

These remarks in regard to the death of animals and the tree of life, have been made, not because they belong to millennarian views; *for they do not;* but for the purpose of meeting some difficulties which have been urged against the idea of a complete restoration of man, and creation, animate and inanimate, to Eden purity, blessedness, and immortality.

What, it is asked, will you do with animals? Are they to be restored to immortality? By no means.

It is not supposed that animals of any class will be restored to immortal life, for they never possessed it. In regard to them, nature will take its course, as designed of Heaven, and if not destroyed or consumed as food for others, having fulfilled their day, and answered the end of their creation, they will pass away, to give place to other generations, just as they undoubtedly would have done had sin never entered our world.

The race of man, it is believed, will be restored to immortality, when God's scheme of mercy shall be perfected on earth, and as a means, in harmony with the designs of the tree of life in Eden, it is promised that the tree of life shall be restored, whose fruit shall be eaten, and whose leaves shall be for the healing of the nations.

"To him that overcometh will I give to eat of the tree of life, which is in the midst of the paradise of God." Rev. 2 : 7.

Rev. 22 : 1–3. "And he showed me a pure river of water of life, clear as crystal, proceeding out of the throne of God and of the Lamb. In the midst of the street of it, and on either side of the river, was there the tree of life which bore twelve manner of fruits, and yielded her fruit every month; and the leaves of the tree were *for the healing of the nations.* And there shall be no more curse," or death.

It is quite certain that this describes a state of things on earth, from the fact, that the leaves of the tree of life are for the healing of the nations. Now where are any nations to be healed, except on earth? Not surely in heaven; for there all are healed, and must be, before they can enter. And besides, the nations do not exist as such in heaven.

These scriptures then must necessarily have respect to a state of things in our world, where nations need to be healed, and from among whom sin and the curse are to be banished.

3

What a beautiful, consistent, and rational idea is here presented! Man lost his immortality physically, by forfeiting, and being debarred from the tree of life.

He is restored to immortality, through Jesus Christ, by a restoration of the tree of life, of which he will be permitted to eat, in the restored state, and live forever.

The same great truth is brought to view in Ezekiel 47 : 12. "And by the river upon the bank thereof, on this side and on that side, shall grow all trees for meat, whose leaf shall not fade, neither shall the fruit thereof be consumed ; it shall bring forth new fruit according to his month, because their waters they issued out of the sanctuary; and the fruit thereof shall be for meat, and *the leaf thereof* for medicine."

The apostle Paul evidently had his eye on this glorious restitution and regeneration of all things, in his description of creation's deliverance in the 8th chapter of Romans, 19–23.

"For I reckon, that the sufferings of this present time are not worthy to be compared with the glory which shall be revealed in us. For the earnest expectation of the creature waiteth for the manifestation of the sons of God. For the creature was made subject to vanity, not willingly, but by reason of him who hath subjected the same in hope. Because the creature itself also shall be delivered from the bondage of corruption, into the glorious liberty of the children of God. For we know that the whole creation groaneth and travaileth together in pain until now: And not only they, but ourselves also, which have the first fruits of the Spirit, even we ourselves groan within ourselves, waiting for the adoption, to wit: the redemption of our bodies."

There is no difficulty or obscurity in this passage, about which commentators have disagreed so much, according to millennarian expectation. The ground was cursed for man's sake, and creation in all its parts was made subject to evil, in many respects, not willingly or as a voluntary agent, but by reason of the purpose of him who hath subjected the same in hope.

Dr. Chalmers, in his Lectures on the Epistle to the Romans, says upon this passage, "There could be no willingness on the part of the ground in that act of which its curse was one of the consequences.

"It could be from no fault of the will in nature, that she was visited with that sore distemper under which she now labors, and whereof she giveth palpable symptoms in the volcano, and the earthquake and the storm, and the general conspiracy of all her elements, against which man has to fight, and to fatigue himself his whole life long—that he might force out a subsistence and keep footing through a history that is made up of little better than to drudge and to die. It was not of its own willingness that the creation was thus brought under the power of vanity—that at the fall of man, a universal blight came upon nature, by reason of which she is now become a wreck of what she was, still lovely in many of her aspects, though in sore distress—still majestic and venerable, though a venerable ruin—appearing as if out of joint, and giving token by her extended deserts, and the gloom of her unpeopled solitudes, and her wintry frowns, and her many fierce and fitful agitations, that some mysterious ailment hath befallen her; so that the whole passage may be thus paraphrased.

"The creation is now waiting, as if in the attitude of earnest expectancy, for that era, when transformed into a new heaven and a new earth, it shall become a suitable habitation for those who are declared and manifested to be the sons of God.

"For creation then to be so gloriously restored, it has for a time been made subject to vanity, not willingly but by reason of him, who by his fatal disobedience has brought it into this bondage—yet it is a bondage mingled with hope, because creation also shall be delivered from the bondage of corruption: and emancipated from those fetters which now bind and burden, and make it impracticable and ungracious, it will come forth in smiles that shall be perennial, and immortal—it will yield a grateful compliance to the wishes of its happy inmates—and have in all its operations the beneficent flow and freedom of God's own children."

It is clear from this, that the great and good Chalmers did not contemplate the destruction of our world; but its complete restitution, intelligent, animate and inanimate, from all the curse and consequences of sin, to the purity, the peacefulness and blessedness, in which it would have existed had sin never entered.

And how perfectly simple, beautiful, and harmonious, with this great idea of the restoration of all things, is this description of the apostle! How bright and joyous the vision for our world! Cowper felt the inspiration of its glory when he wrote the following lines:

"O scenes surpassing fable, and yet true!
Scenes of accomplished bliss! which who can see,
Though but in distant prospect, and not feel
His soul refreshed with foretaste of the joy?
Rivers of gladness water all the earth,
And clothe all climes with beauty; the reproach
Of barrenness is past. The fruitful field
Laughs with abundance; and the land, once lean,
Or fertile only in its own disgrace,
Exults to see its thistly curse repealed.
The lion, and the leopard, and the bear,
Graze with the fearless flocks; all bask at noon
Together, or all gambol in the shade
Of the same grove, and drink one common stream.
Antipathies are none. No foe to man
Lurks in the serpent, now. The mother sees,
And smiles to see, her infant's playful hand
Stretched forth to dally with the crested worm
To stroke his azure neck, or to receive

The lambent homage of his arrowy tongue.
The creeping pestilence is driven away;
The breath of heaven has chased it. In the heart
No passion touches a discordant string,
But all is harmony and love. Disease
Is not: the pure and uncontaminated blood
Holds its due course, nor fears the frost of age.
One song employs all nations; and all cry,
Worthy the Lamb, for he was slain for us!
The dwellers in the vales, and on the rocks,
Shout to each other, and the mountain-tops
From distant mountains catch the flying joy
Till, nation after nation taught the strain,
Earth rolls the rapturous hosanna round."

Such, then, is the sense in which millennarians expect the conversion of the world, an entire restoration of man, and of creation, animate and inanimate, to holiness, prosperity and happiness forever.

The grand idea is that conceived by Milton, in his two poems, "Paradise Lost;" "Paradise Restored." How beautiful, and grand, and sublime the thought! How infinitely more exalted, and God-like, than the views of those who believe that sin will exist in our world up to the end of time, and that men must, until the winding up of all human things, pursue their way through sorrow and tribulations to the world to come.

And now, what is there unreasonable in these views of the restitution of all things, so clearly taught in Scripture? Is it unworthy of Jesus thus to regenerate and restore the world in all its parts? Is it, in any way, contradictory to his infinite love and blood-bought righteousness, thus to destroy the works of the devil—thus to annul the curse—thus to wipe out the reproach of earth, and bring it back to that purity and blessedness in which it was when it came from the forming hand of God? And is it in any way impossible that he should do it? Are not his love, wisdom, and power united, adequate to the glorious task? And what a mighty triumph it would be over all the powers of darkness! What a wondrous spectacle to the universe thus to see earth redeemed and restored! Would not such a work be infinitely worthy of God, and sublimely illustrative of his love which is unsearchable? So we believe, and so we teach.

"Haste, then, and wheel away a shattered world,
Ye slow-revolving seasons! We would see
A sight to which our eyes are strangers yet,
A world that does not dread and hate his laws,
And suffer for its crime; would learn how fair
The creature is that God pronounces good;
How pleasant in itself what pleases him."

And when this restoration is perfected, we expect, on truly Scriptural grounds, that our earth will abide forever, a monument of redeeming love, and that the redeemed and sanctified nations who shall live and be born therein, having fulfilled their happy lot and destiny in life, will be transfigured to the glorified without seeing death, as was Enoch and Elijah, to make room for others who came after them in endless succession.

Reader, turn not up the lip at this, nor dismiss it as absurd, until you have examined our scriptural arguments and deductions. You must admit that it is no mean and contemptible idea we entertain of the grace of God, and the boundless extent of his salvation. Let it be borne in mind, then, as we proceed, that the grand idea of Millennarianism is the salvation of the world—a complete restoration of all things. All that follows are only the agents, means and instrumentalities by which it is to be accomplished. But when will this great and glorious restoration, spoken of by all God's holy prophets, be accomplished? Not, certainly, during the prevalence of the present gospel dispensation. But why? Cannot God convert the world now, as well as at any future period? Cannot he so bless the means and agencies now employed, and so accompany them with the outpourings of his Spirit, as to accomplish all that is predicted before the end of this dispensation? Do you deny, or limit, or undervalue the means of grace which God has appointed, or repudiate the efficacy of the gospel, or the influences of the ever-blessed Spirit? By no means. We would not dare place any limits to any of these which God has not himself placed in his revealed Word, nor do we undervalue his Spirit, or suppose that his glorious gospel will ever be thrown aside, or fail to accomplish all that was contemplated in the counsels of eternal love. But these are not the questions. The point is, what has God taught? If he has ever said that the latter day glory, predicted in Scripture, is to be brought about, and ushered in by the instrumentalities now employed, and before this dispensation closes, then where is the record? Show us a "thus saith the Lord," and we yield a willing assent to all that is written.

It is not on theoretical or speculative grounds that the position is taken, that the world cannot all be converted during the present economy of the grace of God; but because it is believed that the Scriptures so teach. And—

1. There are various New Testament Scriptures, which represent the gospel at present as only partial or limited in its saving influence on mankind. As, Matt. 7: 13, 14, "Enter ye in at the strait gate: for wide is the gate, and broad is the way which leadeth unto destruction, and many there be which go in thereat: Because strait is the gate and narrow is the way which leadeth unto life, and few there be that find it."

The history of the past and present, shows how literally and truthfully these scriptures describe the actual results of the gospel. Will the results ever be different during the prevalence of the present dispensation?

Has the Saviour ever said or intimated, that the time will

come, before the present dispensation closes, when the broad way will be forsaken, and all press the narrow way?

Now, the world cannot be all converted, while these scriptural representations are true or in force: for if all were converted, it could not be said, "Wide is the gate, and broad is the way which leadeth unto destruction, and many there be which go in thereat." We therefore conclude, that as our Lord has placed no limit to the signification of these scriptures before the end of the present dispensation, they were designed to represent a state of things to continue until its end, and that the conversion of the world must be at a period after the era for which these partial representations were designed.

In harmony with the above, is the parable of the sower, Matt. 13, which was designed to represent the constant effects of the preaching of the gospel up to the end of the dispensation.

The sower ever goes forth to sow. The scattered seed ever falls, some by the way side, some on stony places, and some among thorns, and produces no fruit. This correctly represented the effects of the gospel in the time of our Lord and his apostles; it has in every age of the world since; it does now. Will it not continue to do so until the end of the dispensation? Has the Saviour ever said it will not? Has he ever limited its signification to a part of this dispensation, or said that the time will come, when for a thousand years or more before the end, the seed sown will all, or the most of it, fall on good ground, and produce its appropriate fruit?

Now it is manifest that the glowing predictions of the Old Testament prophets cannot be fulfilled in the conversion of the entire world to God, nor yet Christ destroy the works of the devil, and cause the will of God to be done on earth as it is in heaven, while these scriptures which limit the saving influences of the gospel are in force. Any one may see that the conversion of the entire world would render these scriptures incorrect representations of the actual state of things then existing.

But these scriptures are manifestly designed to represent the whole career of this dispensation; because our Lord has placed no limit to them before the end, and therefore no one else has a right to: and hence it is inferred, that if the world is ever converted, as it must be according to the prophets, the grand results must be obtained in some new dispensation, to which these scriptures, which limit the saving influences of the gospel, do not apply. But,

2. To say that all those scriptures which predict the entire conversion and restoration of our world, will be fulfilled during the present dispensation, is to make them clash with, and contradict all those New Testament scriptures which represent and teach that the church and the world will continue to exist in a corrupt and mixed state up to the end of the world or dispensation; and hence such an exposition and application of these prophesies cannot be true.

"By the parable of the tares and wheat," Matt. 13, we are taught that the world is like a field in which a man sowed good seed, and his enemy sowed tares. The good seed are the children of the kingdom; and the tares are the children of the wicked one. Both the tares and the wheat, by the command of the Lord of the field, must be permitted to grow together till the harvest, which is interpreted to signify the end of the world, or more properly the dispensation, as the original word confirms.

However largely and widely then the sowers of the good seed may scatter it, and however abundantly God may bless the labor, still the enemy is not less industrious. The tares he sows will continue to spring up and grow, commingled with the wheat until the end.

The obvious design of this parable cannot be mistaken. As the parable of the sower represents the effects of the gospel at any one time wherever it is preached, so the parable of the tares represents the continued moral aspects of the world under the influence of preaching from age to age, till the end of the dispensation.

The same general truth is brought to view in the parable of the net and fishes. The world is to exist in a mixed state, and the gospel net is to gather good fish and bad until the end, when the angels are sent forth to sever the wicked from among the just. And the wise and foolish virgins are to remain mingled in the church until the coming of the Bridegroom.

Now these words of our Lord, communicated in these parables, are true and faithful, and every jot thereof shall be fulfilled.

Can any tell, then, how the tares can grow with the wheat until the end of the world—how the gospel net can catch good fish and bad; and the foolish virgins exist and mingle with the wise until the coming of the Son of Man; and yet the world all be converted, and all be righteous for a thousand, or thousands of years before the end? The thing is impossible. Our Lord being the judge and interpreter, the world cannot all be converted and restored, and the will of God done on earth as it is in heaven, before the end of the present dispensation; because he has taught in these parables that it shall not so be fulfilled.

All these scriptures were designed to extend to the end; and to say, then, that the gospel is yet to gradually expand into the "noon-tide glory of the millennial day" during this dispensation, is to bring all the prophesies referring to the conversion of the world, in direct contradiction to these New Testament statements of doctrines and facts; and, therefore, such an application must be unscriptural and untrue. But all difficulties here are avoided, if the scriptures justify the idea of a new dispensation beyond the end of the present, in which all that the prophets have foretold shall be accomplished.

3. It is argued that the Old Testament prophesies cannot be fulfilled in the conversion of the entire world to God, before the end of this present dispensation; because, neither the Saviour, nor his apostles, ever distinctly pointed to this, or foretold it, as one of the great and grand events which was to precede his second coming. I have searched in vain for any such intimation.

Reader, did you ever see or hear of a passage, in which it was distinctly stated that the world would be converted before the second glorious appearing of our Lord?

But why this silence upon a subject so vast and important, if true? When our Lord was inquired of by his disciples, when shall these things be? and what shall be the sign of thy coming, and of the end of the *aion* or dispensation? He told them in reply, that "There shall be signs in the sun and in the moon, and in the stars; and upon the earth distress of nations with perplexity; the sea and the waves roaring; men's hearts failing them for fear, and for looking after those things which are coming upon the earth: for the powers of heaven shall be shaken. And then shall they see the Son of man coming in the clouds of heaven with power and great glory."

He gave them to understand that the dispensation which was to precede his second advent, would be marked, in respect to the Jews especially, as a time of prolonged and unprecedented trouble; and by wars and rumors of wars among the nations until the end. But never did he whisper a word about the world's conversion.

Now if such a conversion, as many expect, when, for a long period before the end, righteousness is to prevail, is true, it is undoubtedly one of the most grand and glorious events which is to precede the coming of the Son of man.

And if so, is it not strange that our Lord did not mention, or allude to it as a most prominent event? And is not his entire silence presumptive proof, at least, that no such event as the world's conversion is to take place before his own glorious appearance in our world a second time, without sin unto salvation?

Nor did the apostles ever mention the conversion of the world, in all their predictions concerning the last times, as an event to occur before the coming of the Lord.

They tell of apostacies, of the rise of Antichrist, and of the prevalence of great and terrible wickedness; but never of the reign of universal holiness and happiness, during the present economy. Our Lord and his apostles never held up the conversion of the world as the great and grand incentive to benevolent effort. Their silence has a portentous meaning, and proves that the world is not, according to scripture, to be converted and restored, as predicted, during the existence of the present dispensation. I see not how to avoid this conviction or conclusion.

4. But especially, and above all, it is believed that the conversion and restoration of our world is reserved for a new economy or dispensation to be introduced at the termination of the one under which we now live; because the scriptures so teach most clearly and harmoniously. The proof of this will be presented in the next chapter, to which the attention of the reader is respectfully directed.

The present dispensation, which according to our Lord's teaching is to be one of a mixed character up to the end, and also one of suffering and trial till its close, was never expected to result in the conversion of all.

Its object is clearly set forth by the apostle in Acts 15: 14. "Simeon hath declared how God at the first did visit the Gentiles to take out of them a people for his name."

And this agrees with the declaration of Christ, Matt. 24:

14, "And this gospel of the kingdom shall be preached in all the world, for a witness unto all nations; and then shall the end come."

Also with the great commission given to the apostles: "Go ye into all the word and preach the gospel to every creature: he that believeth and is baptized shall be saved, and he that believeth not shall be condemned." Some have maintained, that in the commission to preach the gospel to all, there is an implied promise that the world will all be converted, as the result.

But not so. The limiting and qualifying enactment accompanying it, shows that the conversion of the entire world was not contemplated as the result of publishing it as a witness to all nations. "He that believeth shall be saved, but he that believeth not shall be condemned."

Now, the reader will not understand us as opposed to missionary operations at home and abroad.

No, God bless Bible Societies, and Missionary Societies, and Tract Societies, and the good and devoted men who conduct and patronize them. They are engaged in a great and holy cause, and have been raised up in providence to accomplish his purpose in publishing the gospel to all nations as a witness, and in gathering that great multitude out of every nation, and kindred, and people, and tongue under heaven, to whom the government of the kingdom is to be given. Their labor shall not be in vain in the Lord; for his word shall not return unto him void, but it shall accomplish that which he has designed, and prosper in the thing whereunto he has sent it.

Do we oppose missions because we maintain, in accordance with the scriptures, that all will not be converted during the present economy? What devoted minister now preaches with the expectation of saving all to whom he ministers? Are his labors therefore in vain?

There are three great motives presented in the New Testament, which bind every child of God to do all he can to send the gospel to the nations, and to save all he can:

1. The command of Jesus—Go ye into all the world, &c. 2. The constraining love of Christ. 3. Love to dying man.

And now may not the millennarian be influenced by all of these, as sincerely as others? May he not consistently with his belief and expectation respect and obey the command of his Lord? May he not love his Saviour as ardently as others, and yearn over dying men with as true and deep a sympathy as they who ridicule the truth he holds as sacred? Why will good men misrepresent and pervert our views, and charge their illogical deductions, drawn from perversion and prejudice, to our account? Many of the most devoted missionaries, such as the murdered Lowrie was, and the laborious Poor of Ceylon now is, have been millennarians, and have testified that their views did not diminish, but ministered to their missionary zeal.

Chapter Third.

THE MILLENNIUM, A NEW DISPENSATION—DURING WHICH THE WORLD IS TO BE CONVERTED, AND THE RESTITUTION OF ALL THINGS TO TAKE PLACE.

It has been shown that the world cannot be converted and restored during the present dispensation, according to its revealed purpose, and the teachings of our Lord ; that it is to exist in a mixed and corrupt form, even unto the end, when the angels shall sever the wicked from among the just, and the righteous then shine forth as the sun in the kingdom of their Father.

The restoration of all things, it is believed, is reserved for a new dispensation, which will open in effulgent splendor on the world at the termination of the present.

In this new economy, the Old and New Testament prophecies will receive their full and most joyous accomplishment, without contradicting other scriptures, or clashing with the doctrines and statements of our Lord and his apostles.

But what is a dispensation? and what is to be understood by a new one? To allay any fearful apprehensions that some new way of salvation is contemplated, in which prophets and apostles never walked, we would definitely state in the outset, that by a new dispensation is not understood a new church, or a new mode of saving men, or any new foundation, other than that which is laid, which is Jesus Christ.

The term dispensation, as indicated by the original word, denotes a particular economy, or arrangement of things, ac-according to which the affairs of a household, or a government, are administered.

In the administration of his church in the world, God has been pleased to pursue different methods in revealing his truth, and in accomplishing the great purposes of his love and wisdom.

These different methods of bestowing his grace and truth are called dispensations. The number of dispensations under which the Church has been placed, from Adam down, has been variously estimated; but there have certainly been three —the Patriarchal, the Jewish, and the Christian.

In regard to these dispensations, two things especially are true, and common to them all.

1. God's method of justifying or saving men through an atoning sacrifice—the Lamb slain in purpose, from the foundation of the world, is the same under each. Abel and Noah, Moses and David, Isaiah and Malachi, and Paul and the whole perfected company of the redeemed, will unitedly ascribe their salvation unto him that loved them and washed them from their sins in his own blood. And in accordance with the same plan, and through the sanctifying influences of the Spirit, we expect that men will be saved in the millennium.

2. Each successive dispensation has been marked by new and more full revelations of truth, and by the establishment of new institutions, by which former laws and ceremonies have been set aside, to give place to that which was more perfect and glorious. Thus the Jewish set aside the Patriarchal, and the Christian or Gospel dispensation has wholly abrogated the Jewish or Mosaic.

In each of these succeeding dispensations, the Church and the world have been placed under new circumstances of trial and discipline, differing in many respects materially from that which preceded.

Though the Church, under the Jewish and Christian dispensations is the same, yet those who live under the Gospel, from the superior light enjoyed, and the more simple and spiritual ritual to be observed, are placed in more favorable circumstances, in respect to the kingdom of God, than those who lived in former ages. Many prophets and righteous men, said the Saviour, have desired to see those things which ye see, and have not seen them; and to hear those things which ye hear, and have not heard them.

Judging from God's dealings in the past, and from his prophetic annunciations respecting the future, it seems clearly to be his established method—his fixed plan, to carry his church through successive developments, from glory to glory, until all his purposes of mercy are accomplished.

There is nothing then contrary to the analogy of God's dealing's with his church heretofore, to suppose that there will yet be another dispensation after the present, in which the world will be placed in still higher and more favorable circumstances of grace and glory than are now enjoyed, and in which new revelations may be made, corresponding to the new order of things, and the fuller developments of love.

In fact, this is just what we might rationally expect from all that God has done, and has purposed to do for our world.

Many good men have often felt the need of some more powerful divine manifestations than have ever yet been experienced, to give the truth an all-controlling and subduing influence over the minds of men, and to scatter forever the film of error and sin which gathers over the mental and moral vision. Such manifestations, it is believed, will be made in a new economy, distinctly foretold in scripture, when means and agencies, appropriate and God-like, will be introduced, designed and adapted to bring every thought and feeling into subjection to Jesus Christ.

Now if God has promised, and will vouchsafe to accomplish all these things in their time, who can doubt or deny that there is marked out in the prophecies a career of glory and blessedness for our miserable world, which must infinitely transcend all that the human mind has ever conceived?

To establish the truth of a new dispensation during the millennium, it will be necessary to show,

1. That the world will be placed, during this period, in such entirely new and different circumstances, that many parts of the New Testament scriptures will be rendered entirely unsuited to the times, and untrue in respect to the state of things which will then exist. And that the light and privileges then to be enjoyed will be far more glorious than are now possessed, or than earth has ever before known. And—

2. That it will be introduced by such marked interpositions of the power and providence of God; and the fulfillment of such predictions respecting Christ and his saints, and the world, as to mark it off as an entirely new and distinct era or economy in the history of the church. Let these positions now be tested by the word of God. And—

1. It is maintained, not only by millennarians, but by most who are not, and who believe in the conversion of the world, that Satan will be bound, or excluded from any evil influence over the world, during the millennium. This, then, is held as cordially by many who are spiritualists as others: and it is scriptural and reasonable: for how can the world ever be converted while he is permitted to sow tares among the wheat, and left as a roaring lion to go about seeking whom he may devour?

According to this, throughout all the happy years of the millennium, he will not be permitted to tempt nations to sin, or individuals to ruin.

But when this blessed period arrives, what will become of all those portions of scripture which warn us against his subtilty, power, and temptations? What of those which direct us to the armor and the means we must employ in resisting and repelling his assaults?

Here, then, by the very binding of Satan and his dejection to the pit, during the thousand years, large portions of scripture will be entirely superseded, and have no application to the world as it will then exist: for how could a minister preach then from this text, "Be sober, be vigilant, for your adversary the devil as a roaring lion goeth about seeking whom he may devour?" or this, "Put on the whole armor of God that ye may be able to stand against the wiles of the devil, for we wrestle not against flesh and blood," &c.?

Would there be any applicability, then, to all such scriptures, when there was no devil on earth to tempt or fear?

And besides these which speak directly of the devil and his agency there are many promises, and exhortations given to sustain believers under the persecutions, and trials, and evils, prompted or inflicted by Satan, which are now of great weight and importance; but which will have no force in the times and circumstances of those then living. Now we beg the reader to consider, that it is no invention, or speculation of millennarians, which banishes the devil from the world during the millennium, and which consequently declares that all those scriptures which have respect to the devil and his agencies will have expired by their revealed limitation.

The world will then be placed, in this respect, under entirely new and more favorable circumstances of salvation, than now exist or ever have. Who can imagine what a world this will be, when this one prolific source of moral evil and ruin is removed from the sphere of the living? The binding of Satan then alone, with all the multiplied causes for good which will necessarily follow, will clearly indicate the introduction of an entirely new economy in our world.

But these scriptures which have reference to the devil and his agencies, are only a small portion of the word of

God which will be superseded by the circumstances in which the world will be placed during the millennial age.

When the knowledge of the glory of God shall cover the earth, as the waters cover the sea—when every knee shall bow, and tongue confess that Christ is Lord—when all shall be righteous, and all press the narrow way that leads to life, and none have cause to say to his brother or neighbor, know the Lord, as the prophets foretell; what will become of the Saviour's declaration, "wide is the gate, and broad is the way which leadeth to destruction, and many there be which go in thereat: and strait is the gate, and narrow is the way which leadeth unto life, and few there be that find it?" Will these representations be any longer true?

How would a minister preach in the midst of a converted world, from this passage, "strive to enter in at the strait gate: for many I say unto you shall seek to enter in and shall not be able?" or this, "For many are called, but few are chosen?" or, "Ye will not come unto me that ye may have life?" or this, "And this is the condemnation, that light is come into the world, and men love darkness rather than light because their deeds are evil?"

What will become of these, and many similar texts, when all know and love the Lord? Will they be any longer true or applicable to men? Will they not, in fact, when the millennium arrives, have expired by this statute of limitation?

And what too will become of the parable of the sower, when the seed sown all falls into good ground? What of the parable of the tares and wheat? of the net and fishes? and of the ten virgins? When this latter-day glory shall shine in full-orbed, and meridian splendor on the world, and there are no more tares, or bad fish, or foolish virgins?

These and all similar parables, now most correctly represent the progress of the gospel, and the state of things in our world; but they will not, amid the shoutings of a ransomed and restored world.

By the fulfillment of the predictions referring to this period, and by the very circumstances in which a converted world will then be placed, they will be rendered untrue, and unsuited to the times, and will in fact have expired by the ending of the dispensation to which they belonged. When all are converted—all righteous, they can have no more reference to the state of the world than the old Levitical law does to us now.

They may be, and probably will be read, with great profit, as showing the things that are past; and hence, by comparison, may be the means of showing the preëminently exalted privileges and blessings of those who shall live in that pure age, and of exciting the liveliest gratitude and joy; just as the Christian now may be greatly benefitted and instructed by a study of the old Levitical laws, though they have been abrogated by the introduction and revelations of the Christian dispensations under which he lives.

Upon a careful examination and comparison of Old Testament and New Testament scriptures, it will be found that the prophecies respecting the conversion of the world cannot be fulfilled without annulling a great portion of the latter.

The great principles of the divine law, and of the gospel, which must and will run through all dispensations, will of course remain immutable through eternal ages; but those applications of truth which have reference to a corrupt world, mingled with Satan and sin, can have no place when all these are removed.

Now by admitting a new dispensation, we do not bring the prophecies respecting the millennium in collision with those New Testament scriptures, as do those who maintain that all are to be fulfilled under the present gospel economy. We give these New Testament scriptures their full force up to the limits assigned them—the end of the *aion*, or dispensation; and then beyond, amid the glories of a latter day, when Satan and sin shall be banished, we look for all that prophets amid visions of glory have foretold.

There will exist then a necessity for new laws and revelations in the new economy, adapted to the higher state of perfection and blessedness enjoyed. And it is clearly affirmed that these will be given, in that beautiful description of the last days found in Isaiah 2: 2–6. "And many people shall go and say, come ye, and let us go up to the mountain of the Lord, to the house of the God of Jacob; and he will teach us his ways, and we will walk in his paths: for out of Zion shall go forth the law, and the word of the Lord from Jerusalem."

This shows that when the exalted and happy period here predicted arrives, there will be some new laws from heaven, some clearer illuminations of eternal truth, by means of which the peaceful results mentioned in the prophesy are to be accomplished, when nation shall not lift up sword against nation, nor learn war any more.

And, oh, how will war and controversy die, and error and delusion disappear, and truth and love roll as waters of life over the world, before the effulgence of truth beaming from the Lord himself, when that new era shall dawn upon the world, and upon mount Zion, the Lord reigns with his ancients gloriously!

The fact, then, that during the millennium the world will be placed in such entirely new and different circumstances, that many of the New Testament scriptures will be unsuited to the times, and untrue in respect to the state of things which will then exist, *furnishes* a strong argument for a new dispensation in the millennial age: for, "It must be admitted that a state of things which supersedes a part of divine revelation, hitherto enjoyed, and introduces men into a state of things which is the consummation of that revealed, has one grand characteristic of a new dispensation: if not, then the introduction of the Christian era was not a new dispensation, but merely a continuation of the Mosaic."

2. Another argument for a new dispensation is derived from the parables of the tares and wheat, and the net and fishes.

Our Lord, in his exposition of the parable of the tares, says, the good seed are the children of the kingdom, and the tares are the children of the wicked one. The tares must grow with the wheat until the harvest. The harvest is the end of the world, and the reapers are the angels.

There are two words translated world in this parable, which are very different in their signification, κοσμος and αιων, *Kosmos* and *aion.* The kosmos is the earth—the material world in which, or on which men live, and where the wheat and tares are sown. Now it is not said that the harvest is the end of the kosmos—the material world; but the end of the aion—the age, or dispensation.

It is a great mistake, then, to suppose that the harvest is literally at the end of the material world, and the closing up of all human things on earth. The word *aion* stands not in scripture uniformly for the earth; but more commonly for an age or dispensation. Thus in 1 Corinthians 10: 11, it is said, "Now all these things happened unto them for ensamples," that is unto the Israelites in the wilderness; "and they are written for our admonition, upon whom the ends of the world are come, τα τελη των αιωνων, that is, they are written for us who live at the juncture, or ends of the dispensations. The apostles and all of their time lived at the consummation—the end or winding up of the Jewish dispensation, so that upon them, or in their times, the end of the dispensation had come. This is obviously the meaning of the passage, for in no other sense did they live at the end of the world, and in this they did.

Hebrews 9 : 26. "But now once more at the end of the world, hath he appeared to put away sin by the sacrifice of himself." The original is here the same as in the former passage, and has reference simply to the ending or consummation of the levitical dispensation. Christ appeared at the time of the consummation of this, to put an end to sacrifices for sin, by the offering up of himself without spot to God. In no other sense is it true that he appeared at the end of the world.

This special sense of *aion*, coincides, says Robinson, with classic usage.

No violence, therefore, is done to the language, or to scriptural usage, in assigning this meaning, the end or consummation of the dispensation to συντελ εια του αιωνος, the *aion* in the parables. The harvest then is the end, not of the kosmos, but of the dispensation—of that one under which we live.

And as the tares are not gathered out from among the wheat until the harvest, nor the good fish separated from the bad until the end of the present age, the harvest and end must precede the millennium.

From the necessity of the case, we are compelled to give these parables this interpretation and limitation. When all the world is fully and perfectly converted, and Satan and all his children confined to the pit, there will be no more tares or bad fish here to be gathered from among the good.

When the will of God is done on earth as it is in heaven, and all love and serve the Lord in the perfection of the millennial age, the tares will have been all rooted up by the command of the Lord of the harvest.

These parables cannot hence refer to the last acts of

judgment, when the dead, small and great, shall stand before God ; because the righteous and the wicked are, in respect to the dead, separated at death.

The kingdom of God, for which we are taught to pray, is in this world, and it is out of this kingdom that the tares, the children of the wicked one, are to be gathered ; for there is no other kingdom in which they exist, mingled with the good, except on earth. And when this takes place, then, indeed, will the righteous shine forth as the sun, in the kingdom of their Father.

While these parables, therefore, and all similar scriptures, show that the world will not be converted according to God's appointment during the prevalence of that dispensation, through the entire length of which they are to have full force, they harmonize most perfectly with millennarian views, which provide for the rich abounding mercy of God to the world, in due time, without attempting to mar the symmetry of the gospel, or to stretch this dispensation beyond its revealed limits. And they show that, if our lost world is ever restored, it must be in a new dispensation which comes after the end to which they refer.

3. A third argument in proof that the millennium will be a new dispensation, and will exist under an entirely new constituted order of things, is inferred from Isaiah 65 : 17, 19, 25, and parallel passages :

"For behold, I create new heavens and a new earth : and the former shall not be remembered, nor come into mind. But be ye glad, and rejoice forever in that which I create ; for behold I create Jerusalem a rejoicing and her people a joy. And I will rejoice in Jerusalem, and joy in my people: and the voice of weeping shall no more be heard in her, nor the voice of crying. There shall be no more thence an infant of days, nor an old man that hath not filled his days ; for the child shall die an hundred years old ; but the sinner being an hundred years old, shall be accursed. And they shall build houses and inhabit them; and they shall plant vineyards, and eat the fruit of them. They shall not build, and another inhabit; they shall not plant, and another eat; for as the days of a tree are the days of my people, and mine elect shall long enjoy the work of their hands. They shall not labor in vain, nor bring forth for trouble; for they are the seed of the blessed of the Lord, and their offspring with them. And it shall come to pass, that before they call, I will answer; and while they are yet speaking, I will hear. The wolf and the lamb shall feed together, and the lion shall eat straw like the bullock; and dust shall be the serpent's meat. They shall not hurt nor destroy in all my holy mountain, saith the Lord."

Isaiah 56: 22, 23. "For as the new heavens and the new earth which I will make, shall remain before me, saith the Lord, so shall your seed, and your name remain. And it shall come to pass, that from one new moon to another, and from one sabbath to another, shall all flesh come to worship before me, saith the Lord."

There can be no doubt that these scriptures refer to the millennium—to that "latter-day glory" which, according to prophecy, shall yet dawn upon the world.

The facts and blessedness here described, have never begun to be realized in our world, and they must therefore be future.

But let it be distinctly noticed, that all that is here predicted is to occur under an entirely new constituted order of things—so entirely new, as to be denominated "a new heavens and a new earth."

In introducing the glorious theme, the Lord says, "*For behold*,—mark well what I am about to say,—"For behold, I create a new heavens and a new earth: and the former shall not be remembered nor come into mind." And then, as if to prevent any misunderstanding or misapplication of the language, by referring its fulfillment to some spiritual state in some other world, he immediately adds, " But be ye glad and rejoice forever in that which I create: for behold, I create Jerusalem a rejoicing and her people a joy;" and then he goes on to describe, in detail, a state of blessedness and prosperity on earth, in which houses are built, and vineyards planted, and animals subsist in entire domestication.

Now I see not how language could more clearly or strongly assert the reality of a new dispensation, to be introduced when these glorious predictions, which point to the conversion of our world, are fulfilled. *A new heavens* and *a new earth!* in which the former, by reason of its immense inferiority, shall not be remembered or come into mind! Had God wished to have revealed the reality of a new dispensation, how could he have done it more clearly or directly! What else can answer to the language, or correspond to the description given.

4. The millennium is clearly indicated to be a new dispensation in the fact that it will be introduced to the world by the coming of the Son of man in the clouds of heaven, in some very peculiar sense.

Daniel 7: 13, 14. "I saw in the night visions, and behold, one like the Son of man come with the clouds of heaven, and came to the Ancient of days, and they brought Him near before Him. And there was given unto Him, dominion, and glory, and a kingdom, that all people, nations, and languages should serve Him; His dominion is an everlasting dominion, which shall not pass away, and his kingdom that which shall not be destroyed."

If in a subsequent chapter, this great truth here so clearly announced, is more fully, clearly, and scripturally demonstrated, it will follow conclusively, that that era which is introduced by the personal advent of the Son of man, must be a new dispensation, as sublimely and miraculously introduced as any one preceding.

5. The august, and solemn, and portentous manner in which it will be announced to the world, and to all heaven, by the sounding of the seventh angel of the Revelations, shows that the universal reign of Christ on earth will be a new era or dispensation, as clearly defined and marked off as the Jewish or Christian ever were.

Rev. 11 : 15. "And the seventh angel sounded; and there were great voices in heaven, saying, The kingdoms of this world are become the kingdoms of our Lord, and of his Christ, and he shall reign for ever and ever." How august and grand the announcement! Does it not, in accordance with the considerations already presented, clearly indicate the ushering in of a new economy to our world? And the events described as immediately following this announcement, show that they are altogether unusual, and unexperienced.

"And the four and twenty elders which sat before God on their seats, fell upon their faces and worshipped God, saying, We give thee thanks, O Lord God Almighty, which wast, and art, and art to come; because thou hast taken to thee thy great power, and hast reigned. And the nations were angry, and thy wrath is come, and the time of the dead that they should be judged, and that thou shouldst give reward unto thy servants the prophets, and to the saints, and them that fear thy name small and great; and shouldst destroy them which destroy the earth."

All that is here declared will, we believe, take place at the introduction of the millennial age—the resurrection and reward of the righteous dead, and the destruction of the angered, apostate nation, who will not that the Lord should reign over them. These things will be definitely treated of hereafter; and if such sublime and fearful events are to usher in the redemption of our world, can the era which they announce be less than a new dispensation?

6. In confirmation of the argument thus far presented, there are some passages in the writings of the apostles, upon which the fact of a new dispensation sheds a flood of glorious light.

Eph. 1 : 10. "That in the dispensation of the fullness of times he might gather together in one all things in Christ, both which are in heaven, and are in earth, even in Him." This, according to millennarian views, will be most strikingly fulfilled when Christ, in the coming dispensation, shall gather together all his saints, above and below, raised and transfigured into one glorious and eternal kingdom.

It is thought also by many, that reference is made to this new dispensation in Heb. 2 : 5.—"For unto the angels, hath he not put in subjection the world to come whereof we speak," that is, the new world or dispensation : for this is to be in subjection to the saints. "Know ye not," says Paul, "that the saints shall judge" or rule "the world?" And the prophet Daniel says, "And the kingdom, and the greatness of the kingdom under the whole heaven, shall be given to the people of the most High."

And now what need have we of further testimony? Has any other preceding dispensation clearer or more ample proof to sustain it?

And in conclusion, may it not be asked, what is there unreasonable or unworthy of God, in the idea of a new and more glorious dispensation of his abounding mercy as presented? It is not contended that there will be a new dispensation on the ground that the present one is unsuited to its purpose, or unadapted to accomplish all that God has designed.

By no means. Such an imputation would be an impeachment of the wisdom of the Lord. The present will accomplish all that was contemplated. Not one word of God shall return unto him void, but shall accomplish all that he has designed, and prosper in the thing to which he has sent it.

But if we say that the Jewish dispensation was more glorious than the Patriarchal, and that the Christian is still more clear and glorious than the Mosaic, do we say that the Patriarchal and Mosaic were unsuited to their times, and unadapted to accomplish all the purposes contemplated in their institution? We believe, most assuredly, that they were most wisely adapted to their times and ends; and so we believe that the present is most wisely adapted to its end—to test men, and to gather out of all nations a redeemed people for his name, and to train, and discipline, and sanctify them, and make them meet for the possession of his eternal kingdom. The present dispensation has a great and glorious mission to perform, in preparing the way for the future and everlasting kingdom of God. And it will not have come to an end until its work is fully, and according to divine appointment, done.

But under the present gospel dispensation there exists many and formidable difficulties. Though exceedingly rich in the grace of God, and in the saving and sanctifying influences of his spirit, what errors prevail, and what apostacies! Amid how many difficulties, and corruptions, and opposing powers are men compelled to pass their probation for eternity! What vast multitudes are seduced by the world, the flesh, and the devil, to ruin! What crowds press the downward road, and what dangers and complicated miseries press around men's critical probation for eternity! Is there nothing better in reserve? Will not God in his love, when he has accomplished all his purposes in the present economy, introduce the world to higher privileges and blessings, where, delivered from the temptations of Satan and sin, and freed from all that can hurt or destroy, the generations of men may walk perpetually in the light of God's countenance, and enjoy the full-orbed glories of the Sun of Righteousness, in a new and more glorious economy?

Would such a proceeding be unworthy of God, or derogatory to the glorious triumphs of the Redeemer? Such is the hope which the millennarian derives from the scriptures—such are his ardent anticipations in regard to the triumphs of the kingdom of God on earth. It is a hope full of immortal glory, and sheds a brighter effulgence over Jehovah's name, than does the idea that the present dispensation, mingled with sin, must continue to the winding up of all earthly things, when God, according to a common opinion, will burn up the world as a worn out and an accursed thing. The ideas which the scriptures give us of the infinite and eternal results of the work of Jesus, as infinitely transcend these narrow views as heaven is higher than earth.

But when this new dispensation of the kingdom of God shall be introduced in the manner and form predicted, it is not expected that a complete and perfect restoration of all things, morally and physically, will be effected by a stroke, or in an instant of time; but, on the contrary, some length of time may be occupied in its perfection. We pretend not to say how long it may take to accomplish the end. Though the agencies employed will be most wisely adapted and potent, yet, as God does not work miracles when ordinary means will do the work, the causes then set in operation may be left to work out in regular process their glorious results. And hence it may take hundreds of years to wipe out every stain of sin upon earth, and so perfectly to restore man's physical nature as to annul the curse in every individual. And it is probable that to this period, to the first years of the millennial age, is to be referred the passage in Isaiah 65: 20:

"There shall be no more thence an infant of days, nor an old man that hath not filled his days: for the child shall die an hundred years old: but the sinner being an hundred years old shall be accursed."

This must refer to the first years of the millennium, before the works of the devil, and the curse of sin and death, are wholly destroyed. It cannot characterize the whole period of the kingdom of God, or the new heavens and earth, for it is positively affirmed that there shall be no more curse or sin when the restoration is perfected, therefore there can be no more any death when the curse ceases to operate.

It is furthermore affirmed, that there shall be no more heard the voice of weeping or the voice of crying: but where there are sin and death, there must be both; and hence, in the new heavens and the new earth, when there shall be no more weeping or crying, and when God shall wipe away tears from all faces, there can be no more any sin or death. It is also recorded, that there shall be no more pain, and this shows that there can be no sin or death, when in the new dispensation the restoration is perfected. And then again we are told (Isaiah 25 : 8), that when the Lord of Hosts shall make unto all nations a feast of fat things in Mount Zion, "He will swallow up death in victory; and the Lord will wipe away tears from all faces;" and this demonstrates that when the great blessedness is enjoyed which is promised in this prediction, there shall be no sin, sorrow, or death.

The passage, then, under consideration, must refer to the first years of the new dispensation, while the work of restoration is in progress, and before it is perfected. Viewing the passage in this light, it is rational and entirely consistent with the expectation that, in this new economy, denominated the new heavens and the new earth, there will be an entire restoration of all things, intelligent and unintelligent, animate and inanimate, to Eden's purity, blessedness and immortality.

" The groans of Nature in this nether world,
Which heav'n has heard for ages, have an end,
Foretold by prophets, and by poets sung,
Whose fire was kindled at the prophet's lamp ;
The time of rest, the promised Sabbath, comes,
Six thousand years of sorrow have well nigh
Fulfill'd their tardy and disastrous course
Over a sinful world ; and what remains
Of this tempestuous state of human things
Is merely as the workings of a sea
Before a calm that rocks itself to rest ;
For he, whose cars the winds are, and the clouds
The dust that waits upon his sultry march,
When sin hath roused him, and his wrath is hot,
Shall visit earth in mercy : shall descend
Propitious in his chariot pav'd with love ;
And what his storms have blasted and defaced,
For man's revolt, shall with a smile repair."

Chapter Fourth.

THE SECOND COMING OF CHRIST TO REIGN UPON THE EARTH—WILL IT BE LITERAL AND PERSONAL, AND AT THE INTRODUCTION OF THE NEW DISPENSATION, OR BEFORE THE MILLENNIUM?

The answer to these inquiries cannot be a matter of indifference or of little consequence; for if the second predicted advent of our Lord is pre-millennial, it is a matter of great and practical importance that those, especially, who love his appearing, should rightly understand and act in reference to his coming. If it is not true, it is undoubtedly injurious to advocate it, and if it is truly taught in scripture, it is equally injurious and disastrous to deny it. These questions cannot be settled by prejudice, or by their apparent utility or inutility, in our darkened estimation; but by the revelation of God, correctly understood and appreciated.

It is proposed, therefore, to subject these questions simply to the test of scripture; and if inany sense we err, may God pardon our infirmity, and lead us in the way of truth and righteousness.

In looking to the past, it is manifest that each preceding dispensation which has been or which now prevails on earth, has been introduced by a literal and personal coming of God in some visible manifestation. In Eden the Patriarchal was introduced, and there God appeared to our first parents, and personally placed them under that economy under which they and their descendants lived for many generations.

When this terminated, the Jewish dispensation was introduced by the coming of God on Mount Sinai, in awful solemnity and grandeur, and there amid the manifested insignia of eternal majesty, he proclaimed his own name and law in the hearing of the people. But this dispensation, though so fearfully and impressively introduced, was not designed to continue perpetually ; but was added only for a time, until the promised Messiah should come and herald to the world a brighter era.

Accordingly, when the Levitical terminated, the Christian dispensation was introduced by the coming of God in the flesh, to suffer, and bring in everlasting righteousness, for a guilty world.

So in like manner, we sincerely believe that it is clearly revealed in Scripture, that the new—the millennial dispensation, will be introduced by the coming of God, our Lord Jesus Christ, in the clouds of heaven, as a gloriously triumphant Saviour to subdue all things to himself, and to add this revolted world to his already immeasurably vast dominions, and to restore it to its proper place amid the unnumbered and obedient orbs which circle the throne of heaven.

The grand idea, then, of the pre-millennial advent, is manifestly in harmony with all the past, and, as we hope to show, infinitely worthy of the love and wisdom and exalted dignity of God.

The first passage of scripture which will be adduced to prove the pre-millennial advent, is found in—

Acts 3 : 19–21. "Repent ye therefore, and be converted, that your sins may be blotted out, when the times of refreshing shall come from the presence of the Lord ; And he shall send Jesus Christ, which before was preached unto you: whom the heavens must receive until the times of the restitution of all things, which God hath spoken by the mouth of all his holy prophets since the world began."

It is a settled point, and believed by all evangelical Christians, that Jesus Christ has ascended into heaven, where he now sitteth at the right hand of God, and whence he will come to judge the quick and the dead, at his appearing and kingdom.

Now, we are definitely told in this passage, that the heavens into which he has gone, must receive, or contain him, until a certain time, and that time is, *the times* of the restitution of all things which God hath spoken by the mouth of all his holy prophets since the world began. According to the clear import of this scripture then, it is certain that Jesus Christ will be sent a second time to our world, at these times of restitution spoken of by the prophets.

It has been shown in a former chapter, what is meant by these times of the restitution of all things; and if we search the prophets to learn of what they have so generally and uniformly spoken, we can find no other restitution predicted, but a restoration of our world to holiness, and happiness, and immortality, and of creation, animate and inanimate, to that state in which all would have been had sin never entered our world. This passage, then, furnishes clear and convincing proof of the premillennial advent of our Lord.

2. The same conclusion is reached through a passage found in Matt. 19: 27–28: "Then answered Peter, and said unto him, Behold, we have left all and followed thee; what shall we have therefore? And Jesus said unto them, Verily I say unto you, that ye which have followed me, in the regeneration when the Son of Man shall sit upon the throne of his glory, ye also shall sit upon twelve thrones, judging the twelve tribes of Israel."

The regeneration here spoken of cannot refer to the general judgment at the last day, as that day is commonly understood; for who, then, or what, then, is regenerated? According to common belief, does not probation then end? Are not the righteous then taken away to heaven, and the wicked judged and banished to hell, and the world burned up?

Surely there is no regeneration in all this. With the beatification of the righteous excepted, there is vastly more destruction than regeneration, which means to reform anything into a new and better state.

But if we take this passage as referring to the restitution of all things in our world, as was explained in a former chapter, then all is plain. Our world is yet to be regenerated in all its parts, and all converted to God, so that the will of God shall be done on earth as it is in heaven, and the works of the devil entirely destroyed.

This being the most obvious and natural meaning of the passage, it proves that at the conversion of the world, Christ will sit upon the throne of his glory. His glorious appearing will then take place. He will come a second time without sin unto salvation. And why should he not appear at the introduction of so great and glorious an event as that of a world's complete and eternal redemption?

3. Another argument for the second personal appearing of our Lord before the millennium, is derived from the revealed fact, that the destruction of Antichrist, the man of sin, and all antichristian powers, is to be effected by or in connection with the coming of our Lord.

It is not designed here to enter into the discussion of the question, who is meant by Antichrist or the Man of Sin. Protestant writers have very generally understood the Papacy, including, perhaps, all the nationalized hierarchies by which the Church has been corrupted and become apostate.

But whatever Antichristian confederacies are designated by the Antichrist, the Man of Sin, of scripture, it is certain that these powers cannot exist during the millennium. When all know and serve the Lord, from the least unto the greatest; when every knee shall bow, and tongue confess, that Christ is Lord, and all the kingdoms of this world become the kingdoms of our Lord and of his Christ; everything that opposeth or exalteth itself against God, must necessarily have been removed out of the way.

But if it can be shown that all these Antichristian powers are to be overthrown by or in connection with the personal, visible coming of Christ, it will follow legitimately that his second coming must be pre-millennial.

Let us see. 2 Thess. 2: 1-8. "Now we beseech you, brethren, by the coming of our Lord Jesus Christ, and by our gathering together unto him, that ye be not soon shaken in mind, or troubled, neither by spirit, nor by word, nor by letter as from us, as that the day of Christ is at hand. Let no man deceive you by any means; for *that day* shall not come, except there come a falling away first, and that Man Sin be revealed, the Son of perdition; who opposeth and exalteth himself above all that is called God, or that is worshipped; so that he, as God, sitteth in the temple of God, showing himself that he is God. And now ye know what withholdeth that he might be revealed in his time. For the mystery of iniquity doth already work; only he who now letteth will let, until he be taken out of the way. And then shall that Wicked be revealed, whom the Lord shall consume with the spirit of his mouth, or by his word, and shall destroy with the brightness of his coming."

Now is it not postively affirmed here, that this man of sin, this son of perdition—this wicked one, shall be consumed with the spirit of Christ's mouth, and shall be destroyed with the brightness of his coming?

But what kind of a coming is here meant? Let us turn back and see if we can determine by the connection. In his first Epistle to the Thessalonians, 4: 13-18, we find this record: "But I would not have you to be ignorant, brethren, concerning them which are asleep, that ye sorrow not, even as others which have no hope. For if we believe that Jesus died and rose again, even so them also which sleep in Jesus, will God bring with him. For this we say unto you by the word of the Lord, that we which are alive and remain unto the coming of the Lord, shall not prevent them which are asleep. For the Lord himself shall descend from heaven with a shout, with the voice of the archangel, and with the trump of God: and the dead in Christ shall rise first. Then we which are alive and remain, shall be caught up together with them in the clouds to meet the Lord in the air: and so shall we ever be with the Lord. Wherefore comfort one another with these words. But of the times and seasons, brethren, ye have no need that I write unto you. For yourselves know perfectly, that the day of the Lord so cometh as a thief in the night. For when they shall say, peace and safety, then sudden destruction cometh upon them, as travail upon a woman with child; and they shall not escape."

It is not generally denied, by those who are not millennarians, that a real personal, glorious appearing of our Lord is here intended. It is so uniformly understood and quoted.

From this representation, the Thessalonians very naturally received the impression, that the descent of Christ from heaven was nigh at hand, and perhaps immediately to take place; and hence they were unduly and unnecessarily excited.

This, however, was not true. Christ was not then immediately to appear in the manner and for the purpose described; and his second Epistle seems to have been written for the purpose of disabusing their minds, and giving them some definite instruction as to the time when the glorious appearing of the Son of man might be expected.

But yet it was a great, glorious, and fundamental truth that the Lord was to come again to our world. And hence, before correcting their impressions as to the time when it would take place, he reaffirms the truth, in language most solemn and impressive. 2 Thess. 1: 7–10:

"And to you who are troubled rest with us, when the Lord

Jesus shall be revealed from heaven, with his mighty angels, in flaming fire, taking vengeance on them that know not God, and that obey not the gospel of our Lord Jesus Christ: who shall be punished with everlasting destruction from the presence of the Lord, and from the glory of his power; when he shall come to be glorified in his saints, and to be admired in all them that believe."

Does any true believer doubt that a literal, personal coming of Christ is here intended? Is it not uniformly quoted to prove the second advent of our Lord to judge the world?

Thus far certainly all is plain and undisputed. The apostle is speaking only of a personal and literal coming.

Three verses in advance of this, chapter 2: 1, and in continuation of the same discourse respecting the revelation of Jesus Christ from heaven, he says, "Now we beseech you, brethren, by the coming of our Lord Jesus Christ, and by our gathering together unto him, that ye be not soon shaken in mind, or be troubled, neither by spirit, nor by word, nor by letter as from us, as that the day of Christ is at hand. Let no man deceive you by any means: for that day, that is the day of the Lord's appearing, shall not come, except there come a falling away first, and that man of sin be revealed, the son of perdition, &c."

Now is it not most manifest that the apostle here speaks of the same literal, personal coming, of which he had been speaking all along, and of which he had just reassured them, a personal revelation in flaming fire? It is by this coming that he beseeches them not to be soon shaken in mind, or be troubled, under the impression that it would soon break upon the world. And does not the fact that he declares that the Lord will not come until a great apostacy had occurred, clearly imply that when that was fully revealed or developed, his coming in flaming fire might be expected?

And now then, when he has described this Man of Sin, and

the full revelation of this wicked one, and then declares that he shall be consumed with the spirit of Christ's mouth, and destroyed with the brightness of his coming, does he not manifestly mean the same personal coming of which he had been speaking all along in his first, and in this second epistle? And hence, does it not prove that this Antichristian power is to exist up to the time of the second coming of our Lord, and hence that there will be no universal conversion of the world before he comes?

What other construction can the apostle's language consistently bear? Is it said that the apostate powers here represented, are to be destroyed by their conversion, by Christ's spiritual coming? But whence is such a meaning derived? From the general tenor of Paul's discourse, and the uniform sense in which he speaks of the revelation of the Lord? or from human imagination and invention? Do not the connections of the passage clearly show that the coming by which Antichrist is to be destroyed, is identically the same as that of which he had just before spoken? A literal coming in flaming fire to destroy his enemies, and to be admired in all them that believe?

And what right has any one to say, that in the first part of this Epistle, and in the first verses of this chapter, a personal coming is meant, and that then, without any change in the subject of the discourse, or any notice of the fact, in the course of a few verses he speaks of a coming which is not in fact a coming, and which is as widely different from the literal coming of which he had been all along speaking, as heaven is from earth? Surely, to give without authority from the context or subject, such widely different meanings to the same word, used in the same discourse, and in the same unbroken connection, is to confound all consistency and all certainty in language. What, according to such a mode of interpreting scripture, might not be proved from the Bible?

And the fact that this wicked Antichrist is to be consumed with the spirit of his mouth, does not show that he is to be converted by the Holy Spirit, or that Christ's coming is spiritual.

"The expression, *spirit of his mouth*, is literally the breath or wind of his mouth. There is nothing here which necessarily determines it to mean the Holy Spirit. The spirit of his mouth is not the title of the Holy Spirit, nor is the phrase ever used to denote an influence of the Holy Spirit. It is indeed in one place said that the heavens and all their hosts were made by the breath of his mouth; but the idea is, very obviously, that God created them by his word."

"There are two ideas which the phrase breath or spirit of his mouth may literally express: either a mighty tempest or a mighty voice." "The expression, spirit of his mouth, as used by the apostle here, may literally mean a mighty tempest, or a mighty voice, or both. The apostle, in his first epistle, had said the Lord should descend with a shout; and literally this will be the blast or spirit of his mouth;" when he is revealed from heaven in flaming fire taking vengeance on them who know not God and who obey not the Gospel. And this is all in accordance with prophecy oft repeated.

Isaiah says, 11: 4, of Christ, "And he shall smite the earth with the rod of his mouth, and with the breath of his lips shall he slay the wicked." Again, 30: 28, 30, 33, "And his *breath*, as an overflowing stream, shall reach to the midst of the neck. And the Lord shall cause his glorious voice to be heard, and shall show the lighting down of his arm, and with the flame of a devouring fire. For tophet is ordained of old; yea, for the king it is prepared; he hath made it deep and large; the pile thereof is fire and much wood; *the breath of the Lord*, or the spirit of his mouth, like a stream of brimstone, doth kindle it."

Very many passages might be cited, to show that the phrase, spirit of his mouth, is very commonly employed to denote those destructions and tempestuous judgments upon the wicked which are effected by the word of his power.

So the heavens were made by the word of the Lord, and all the hosts of them by the spirit of his mouth. When the waters of the deluge came up and overpowered the earth, it was effected by the spirit of his mouth. When he commanded the fires to descend on Sodom, the spirit of his mouth as a stream of brimstone did kindle it. And so when God at the judgment shall say to those on his left hand, Depart, &c.—with the spirit or breath of his mouth will he slay the wicked.

And in like manner Antichrist will be consumed by the spirit of his mouth. It will be by the word or command of the Lord that those agencies will be commissioned which will entirely consume and destroy him, at the brightness of his coming.

The sum of the argument then is this. The Antichristian power or powers represented by the man of sin, of which the apostle speaks, must necessarily be destroyed before the millennium; because they cannot exist on earth, when all are converted, and the will of God is done on earth as it is in heaven. But they are all to be destroyed by or at the coming of Christ, personally revealed from heaven, for this purpose among others, to destroy those from the earth who obey not the gospel, and who will not that he should reign over them. The second coming of our Lord, therefore, must be by clear, logical, and unavoidable inference, pre-millennial.

The correctness of the exposition given of the above passage, and of the inference derived, is confirmed by the import and uniform use of the words here translated, the brightness of his coming.

Τη επιφανεια της παρουσιας αυτου. By the epiphany of his

coming, or his appearing and coming. The Greek word, Epiphany, which signifies a glorious appearing, or appearance, always means a personal appearance of the object to which it relates, and when applied to our Saviour, invariably refers to his glorious personal appearing.

It occurs six times in the New Testament, in all of which a literal appearing is always meant.

1 Timothy 6: 14. "That thou keep this commandment without spot, unrebukable, until the *appearing* of our Lord Jesus Christ;" μεχρι της επιφανειας. The commandment here spoken of was not designed for Timothy only, but for all his successors in the ministry until the coming of our Lord. And hence addressed to a whole line or succession of persons, it was to be kept until the epiphany of the Lord.

2 Timothy 1: 10. "But is now made manifest by the *appearing*," the epiphany, "of our Saviour Jesus Christ." This refers to his first advent, which was undoubtedly literal and personal.

2 Timothy 4: 1. "I charge thee therefore before God, and the Lord Jesus Christ, who shall judge the quick and the dead at his *appearing* and kingdom."

2 Timothy 4: 8. "Henceforth there is laid up for me a crown of righteousness, which the Lord, the righteous judge, shall give me at that day; and not to me only, but unto all them also who love his *appearing*;" επιφανειαν.

Titus 2: 13. "Looking for that blessed hope, and the glorious appearing of the great God, even our Saviour Jesus Christ;" επιφανειαν της δοξης.

2 Thess. 2: 8. "And then shall that Wicked be revealed, whom the Lord shall consume with the spirit of his mouth, and destroy with the brightness of his coming," or the glorious epiphany of his coming. In each of the five passages preceding the last, reference is evidently had to the

personal appearance of our Lord. Must it not then in this last passage, especially as the word is never used in any other sense in the New Testament?

The same conclusion is forced upon us, from a consideration of the sense in which the original word translated *coming* is employed in the New Testament; παρουσία. It occurrs twenty-four times in the New Testament, and in every instance refers to the actual appearing or coming of the object referred to. To avoid tediousness, the passages will be omitted, and a reference only made to them in a note.*

Now if in none of the cases in which this word is used, a spiritual or figurative advent of the object to which it relates is meant, but in all cases a literal appearing or coming of the object, must it not denote a personal coming of our Lord in this passage, which declares that that Wicked shall be destroyed by his appearing and coming?

We see not, then, how the conviction can be avoided, that Antichrist is to be destroyed by or in connection with the personal coming of our Lord; and if so, his coming must be pre-millennial.

All this receives additional confirmation, and accords most fully with the fact recorded in the seventh chapter of Daniel, that the power denoted by the Little Horn, which persecutes and wears out the saints of the Most High, is to be destroyed by the Son of man seen coming in the clouds of heaven, to receive the dominion of earth. Dan. 7: 11–14, and 25–27.

It also accords with the events which take place under the sounding of the seventh angel, Rev. 11: 15. "And the seventh angel sounded, and there were great voices in heaven saying, the kingdoms of this world are become the kingdoms

* Matt. 24: 3—24: 27, 37, 39. 1 Cor. 15: 23—16: 17, 2 Cor. 7: 6, 7—10: 10. Phil. 1: 26—2: 12. 1 Thess. 2: 19—3: 13—4: 15—5: 23. 2 Thess. 2: 1—2: 8—2: 9. James 5: 7, 8. 2 Pet. 1: 16—3: 4, 12. 1 John 2: 28.

of our Lord and of his Christ, and he shall reign for ever and ever."

This ushers in the millennium; but it is not the only fact announced: for it is immediately said, "And the nations were angry, and thy wrath is come, that thou shouldst destroy them that destroy the earth." This certainly teaches, that at the time the kingdoms of this world become the kingdoms of our Lord, there will be a destruction of those who receive not the Saviour, and who have destroyed the earth by their errors and persecutions. And who else are likely meant here, by these angered nations, but those Antichristian powers who together constitute the Man of Sin— that Wicked, whom the Lord will consume by the spirit of His mouth, and destroy by the brightness of His coming?

Another remarkable passage, in harmony with the foregoing, is found in Rev. 14 : 6, which shows that at the time the angel is seen in the midst of heaven, having the everlasting gospel to preach unto them that dwell on the earth, and to every nation, and kindred, and tongue, and people, Babylon, the mother of harlots falls, and the Son of man is seen coming on a white cloud, with a drawn sickle in his hand, to reap the earth, and cast it into the wine-press of the wrath of God.

Does not this also clearly assert the destruction of those antichristian confederacies, which are symbolized by the mystical Babylon, at the coming of the Son of man?

All these scriptures evidently point to one and the same thing; and I see not how the conclusion can be avoided, that these Antichristian powers will continue up to the time of Christ's second advent, and then be destroyed, as irreformable and incorrigible, as were the inhabitants of the old world, and of Sodom and Gomorrah.

As all these, then, must be removed before the millennium, and as they are destroyed at the coming of Christ, the argument is conclusive, that his second advent must be pre-millennial.

4. A fourth argument for the personal coming of our Lord before the millennium, and at the establishment of His kingdom in the world, is drawn from the parable of the nobleman. Luke 19 : 11–27.

"And as they heard these things, he added, and spake a parable, because he was nigh unto Jerusalem, and because they thought that the kingdom of God should immediately appear."

He said therefore, "A certain nobleman went into a far country to receive for himself a kingdom, and to return. And he called his ten servants, and delivered unto them ten pounds, and said unto them, occupy till I come. But his citizens hated him, and sent a message after him, saying, We will not have this man to reign over us. And it came to pass when he was returned, having received the kingdom, then he commanded those servants to be called to whom he had given the money, that he might know how much every man had gained by trading," &c.

The apostles evidently believed that Christ had come to set up a great and visible kingdom on earth; and it is a remarkable fact, that if they were in an error in cherishing this expectation, the Saviour never told them so, nor have they ever acknowledged their mistake. If the Lord ever did correct them in this respect, I have been sadly unfortunate in never finding the record of it. But they were in great error in regard to the time of the appearance or setting up of the kingdom; and upon this point our Lord aimed to give them clear and definite instructions; and for this purpose this parable was spoken.

And he added and spoke a parable. What for? Because they had imbibed from their scriptures the absurd idea, that he would at some day receive the throne of his father David, and reign over the house of Israel forever? Not at all. But because they were then nigh unto Jerusalem, and because *they thought* that the kingdom of God should *immediately* appear, and probably supposed that they were going up to Jerusalem for that purpose.

But this was a mistake. His kingdom, which they rightly and scripturally expected, was not immediately to appear; but was to be reserved for a future age or dispensation. To correct their mistake as to the time, and to show them that His kingdom, visibly manifested on earth, was not to be set up until his coming again to our world after his ascension, was the design of the parable.

The nobleman represents our Lord, and his going into a far country to receive for himself a kingdom, and to return, represents his ascension to heaven to receive his kingdom, and his second advent to reign over it, which kingdom, Paul assures, in 2 Tim. 4: 1, is to be manifested at His appearing to judge the living and the dead.

Viewing the parable in this light, which is most natural and obvious, it furnishes a most striking proof and illustration of the second advent of our Lord, at the setting up of his kingdom, or at the introduction of the Millennial age, when He will call together, judge and reward His servants, and destroy those who would not that he should reign over them, agreeably to the statements of the parable.

And according to this interpretation, how admirably adapted was the parable to answer the end designed—to correct their mistake in supposing that he was about to set up his kingdom immediately, and to show them that it was not to appear until after his ascension and return to earth.

5. The evidence thus far presented in proof of the premillennial advent of our Lord, receives additional strength and confirmation, from the revealed fact, that the conversion of the Jews, and their restoration to their own land, which

must take place before or at the commencement of the millennium, are associated in prophesy with some remarkable personal manifestation of the Messiah.

As the conversion and restoration of the Jews will be treated of separately and distinctly in another place, but little will be said here.

Jer. 23: 5–8. "Behold the days come, saith the Lord, that I will raise unto David a righteous Branch, and a king shall reign and prosper, and shall execute judgment and justice in the earth. In his days shall Judah be saved, and Israel shall dwell safely; and this is the name whereby he shall be called, THE LORD OUR RIGHTEOUSNESS. Therefore, behold, the days come, saith the Lord, that they shall no more say, the Lord liveth which brought up the children of Israel out of the land of Egypt; But the Lord liveth which brought up, and which led the seed of the house of Israel out of the north country, and from all the countries whither I had driven them; and they shall dwell in their own land."

The conversion of the Jews in all their wide dispersion, and their final restoration to their own land, are the subjects of discourse in this prediction. But let it be noticed that these take place at the time that the Lord raises up unto David a righteous Branch, who is denominated, The Lord our Righteousness; and who is to execute judgment and justice in the earth.

Interpreters, both Jewish and Christian, concur in the opinion that Christ, the Messiah, is here intended. But a righteous Branch, Jehovah, our Righteousness, has never been raised up to David and Israel in the manner and at the time here predicted. It must, therefore, be yet future.

It could not have been fulfilled before the first advent of our Lord; for Christ did not, and could not become a son of David—a branch growing out of him as a tree or stock, until after his being born in the flesh. It was when he took on him the seed of Abraham, and was born in the line of the family of David, a lineal descendant, that he became a branch unto David and Israel.

Nor was the prophesy fulfilled at his birth, or at his death; for he then came into the world to suffer, not to execute judgment and justice in the land. Nor was it accomplished at his ascension; for, at that time, the children of Israel were not gathered out of all countries into their own land, but were dispersed by the Romans into all nations. Judah was not then saved, nor did Israel dwell safely; but on the contrary their land was then desolated, and their towns and cities burned with fire, and their children slain with the sword; and in no sense did the Lord our Righteousness then execute righteousness and justice in the land as predicted.

That which is here foretold has then never been fulfilled; but it will be at a time when Christ will be raised up to David and to Israel in a peculiar and glorious sense. And what else can be meant here but his personal and glorious appearing to reign over the world, and thus to execute judgment and justice in the land? When this shall take place, we are assured Judah shall be saved, and Israel shall dwell sorely.

A similar passage is found in Jer. 33: 14–16. "Behold, the days come, saith the Lord, that I will perform that good thing which I have promised unto the house of Israel, and to the house of Judah. In those days, and at that time, will I cause the Branch of Righteousness to grow up unto David; and he shall execute judgment and righteousness in the land. In those days shall Judah be saved, and Jerusalem shall dwell safely; and this is the name wherewith he shall be called, *The Lord our* Righteousness. For thus saith the Lord: David shall never want a man to sit upon the throne of the house of Israel." Verses 6–8.—"Behold, I will bring it health and cure, and I will cure them, and will reveal unto them the abundance of peace and truth. And I will cause the captivity of Judah and the captivity of Israel to return, and I will build them, as at the first. And I will cleanse them from all their iniquity, whereby they have sinned against me; and I will pardon all their iniquities whereby they have sinned, and whereby they have transgressed against me."

Here the whole house of Judah and the house of Israel are the subjects of the promise. By a reference to the context, it will be seen that the restoration predicted is to be a restoration from the land of their captivity to Palestine; its mountains and vales, the cities of the south, the cities of Benjamin and Judah, and the whole land that had been desolate.

It is to be attended by their universal sanctification, and universal forgiveness. The time, or period of its accomplishment, is the appearing and the reign of the Messiah on earth; for it is expressly declared, that in *those days*, and at *that time*, the Branch of Righteousness is to grow up, or to appear, and to execute judgment and righteousness in the land.

Nothing like all this was accomplished at the time of our Lord's first coming; for, in connection with that advent, and soon after the ascension of Jesus, destructions wide, wasteful, and terrific, came upon the whole land and nation. And as no conversion, sanctification, and restoration of Judah and Jerusalem have occurred since the ascension of our Lord, the whole prophesy must be yet future.

Now, it is a remarkable fact that whenever the conversion, or restoration of Israel are subjects of prophesy, the promised blessings are frequently associated, in some form, with the manifestation or appearance of Messiah, their king.

Thus the apostle, in speaking of the final universal conversion of the Jews, says—Rom. 11: 26, "And so all Israel shall be saved: as it is written, There shall come out of Zion the *Deliverer*, and shall turn away ungodliness from Jacob"—

thus associating their conversion with the appearing of their Deliverer, Christ.

Now, how strikingly harmonious are all these scriptures with the doctrine of the pre-millennial advent, and reign of Christ on earth! Deny the personal appearing and reign, and you throw a veil of obscurity and utter uncertainty over the meaning of all these prophesies; but admit these, and they seem exceedingly simple and glorious. And hence, in connection with other scriptures, they furnish a clear argument for the pre-millennial advent, and future reign of the Lord our righteousness on earth.

6. That the personal coming of our Lord, is pre-millennial, and for the purpose of reigning upon the earth, is further manifest from all those scriptures, which declare that the Lord God will give unto him the throne of his father David, and that he shall sit upon the throne of David to order it with justice and judgment forever.

When the angel Gabriel announced to Mary the birth of Jesus, he said, Luke 1: 32–33, "He shall be great, and shall be called the Son of the Highest; and the Lord God shall give unto him the throne of his father David. And he shall reign over the house of Jacob *forever*: and of his kingdom there shall be no end."

Isaiah 9: 6, 7.—"For unto us a child is born, unto us a Son is given: and the government shall be upon his shoulders: and his name shall be called Wonderful, Counsellor, the Mighty God, the Everlasting Father, the Prince of Peace. Of the increase of his government and peace there shall be no end, upon the throne of David, and upon his kingdom, to order it, and to establish it with judgment and with justice from henceforth, even forever. The zeal of the Lord of hosts will perform this."

Jer. 23: 15 and 17. In those days and at that time, will I cause the branch of righteousness to grow up unto David;

and he shall execute judgment and righteousness in the land. For thus saith the Lord; David shall never want a man to sit upon the throne of the house of Israel."

The scriptures are many in which a direct mention or reference is made to the fact that Christ shall sit upon the throne of David.

But what do all these mean? In what sense, and when is Christ to occupy the throne of David. He certainly did not when he sojourned in humiliation and sorrow on earth. He does not now, in any conceivable sense, sit upon David's throne, in his exalted and glorified state. He is set down, we are told, with the Father in his throne, and the throne of God was never David's. Jesus now is King of the universe. All power in heaven and in earth is given into his hands, and all made subject unto him, for the salvation of his people, and the accomplishment of his great work in destroying the works of the devil, and in restoring the race of man to holiness and immortality. But this was never David's throne, or government.

Nor will he sit upon David's throne when he comes upon the throne of judgment, to judge the quick and the dead, and assign them their eternal rewards. In what conceivable sense, then, has any government which Christ has ever exercised over angels or men, things visible or invisible, been the government of David? But it is said that as David reigned over the Jews, the people of God, so Christ reigns over the people of God—his spiritual Israel—and in this sense he sits upon David's throne.

But this exposition, in no true sense, meets the conditions of the predictions.

1. David's government was a temporal government over the Jews as a nation. He never was constituted the head of the church, and never did exercise a spiritual government over God's spiritual Israel. But Christ's government over the people of God now is spiritual. He reigns in their hearts by his

spirit, by faith and love. Hence it is, in no conceivable sense, David's throne, which he now occupies in that spiritual government which he exercises in the hearts of true believers: for David never sat upon this throne, and never exercised this government To say that he did, would be to give him the place of God in the hearts of his people, and make him an object of supreme love and worship.

2. The spiritual government which Christ exercises over the people of God commenced with the first believer on earth, and has never since been intermitted, and never will be. Over Abel, and Enoch, and Noah, and the tens of thousands who died in the faith, and went home to heaven, before his first advent, the great Mediator reigned as effectually by his word and spirit, and dwelt in them by faith and love, as over Paul, or the millions who have lived since.

His government over the people of God, then, in this sense, dates back to the first believer, and runs thence downward through all time, and onward through all eternity, and will never terminate while redeemed sinners circle his throne and shout the praises of his love.

But the throne of his father David which was to be given to him, could not be given to him until after his birth: for not until then was he a son of David; and accordingly the promise given to Mary, was not spoken of as a present reality, but as altogether a future thing.

"And he *shall* be great, and shall be called the Son of the Highest; and the Lord God *shall* give unto him the throne of his father David, &c."

The very wording and conditions of the promise show that it was at that time future, and not yet possessed.

Hence it is demonstrable, that the government of Christ spiritually exercised over the true Israel of God, is not the throne of David promised to him: for this government of Christ extends back to the creation, while the throne of David his father, could not be possessed until after he became a son of David by being born unto him in the flesh, and hence was declared to be a still future reality at the time of his birth.

The fact, then, that David reigned over the nominal people of God externally and temporally, does not show that Jesus occupies his throne, in reigning over true believers spiritually, long before David was born, and long since. It would have been extreme trifling to have promised a throne to Christ, which he possessed already, and to style it the throne of David when he never possessed it. To my own mind these prophesies and promises which guarantee to Christ the throne of David, were entirely dark and unintelligible, until the light of Christ's millennial reign dawned upon me.

Now all is plain. When Christ, a son of David according to the flesh—an heir to his throne in regular succession, shall, in the times of the restitution of all things, reign in Jerusalem, where was David's throne, over the restored Jewish tribes, and thence over a redeemed and converted world—the Lord will indeed, then, and in truth have given him the throne of his father David, upon which he will reign forever.

These scriptures, then, furnish clear and striking proof of the pre-millennial advent and reign of Christ on earth.

But when it is said that Christ shall reign in Jerusalem, and upon the throne of David, we do not suppose that he will have a great and splendid palace there, like an earthly monarch, in which he will live, or a gold, or silver, or ivory, throne built, upon which he will sit, in imitation of earthly potentates; but simply that he will there visibly manifest himself in some appropriate and God-like way, which we would not attempt to explain, and there issue his laws, and rule over the children of Israel and the world.

And this is no more unreasonable or undignified, than is the recorded fact, that Jehovah did of old record his name in Jerusalem.

Did he not there dwell in a peculiar manner, and by some visibly manifested glory between the cherubim?

And from thence did he not give forth his oracles, and answer the prayers of his people? And on account of the dwelling of God there, and his visibly manifested glory in the most holy place, did not the pious Jews, wherever they went, turn their faces towards Jerusalem when they prayed?

And may not this have been intended as a type of the more visible, glorious, and enduring manifestation of the incarnate God, in the new dispensation, when not simply to the high priest once a year, in the most holy place, he will show his glory, but openly as he appeared on the mount of transfiguration?

Surely there can be nothing more absurd in the idea of Jehovah Jesus reigning in Mount Zion during future ages, than there was in God's dwelling and reigning there in ancient times.

And as Jehovah's visibly manifested glory there in the most holy place, did not confine him to that one locality, but left him free, as God, to fill the universe with his presence, and heaven with his more immediate smiles, so neither will Christ's reigning in Jerusalem, upon the throne of David, confine him there necessarily, but leave him at liberty to fill and govern his mighty universe according to the counsels of his own will. As God he will still fill all heaven, and in respect to his human form, though it possess not ubiquity, he may transfer it from earth to heaven, or from world to world at pleasure, in company with his glorified saints, and still consistently reign in Mount Zion, and there, at appointed seasons, execute righteousness and justice in the earth. We confess we cannot see the absurdity and groveling sensuality of the reign of Christ on earth which so many sneer at. But—

7. A comparison of what the apostle Peter says in his second epistle, 3 : 13, with what the prophet Isaiah teaches, 65 : 17, and 66 : 22, shows that the coming of Christ must be before the restoration of Jerusalem and conversion of the world.

The apostle Peter, in the third chapter of his second epistle, speaks definitely of the personal coming of the Lord, as a thief in the night for unexpectedness, "in the which the heavens shall pass away with a great noise, and the elements shall melt with fervent heat; the earth also, and the works that are therein shall be burned up."

There can be no doubt that this conflagration takes place after the coming of the Lord. But the apostle goes on to say, "Nevertheless," that is, notwithstanding this general destruction by fire, the world will not be annihilated, but "we, according to his promise, look for a new heavens and a new earth, wherein dwelleth righteousness."

From the connection in which this passage stands, it is manifest that the new heavens and the new earth of which the apostle speaks, come after, and are the result of the Lord's coming, as is evident from the verse following:

"Wherefore, beloved, seeing that ye look for such things, be diligent that ye may be found of him in peace, without spot and blameless. But this new heavens and new earth are the fulfilment of a prophetic promise, for thus it is written, We, according to his promise, look for a new heavens and a new earth, wherein dwelleth righteousness," or in which righteous people will dwell.

Let us turn now to the original promise, and see how it is given, and when it is to be accomplished. Isaiah 65 : 17-19. "For behold, I create new heavens and a new earth; and the former shall not be remembered nor come into mind. But be ye glad, and rejoice forever in that which I create: for behold, I create Jerusalem a rejoicing, and her people a joy. And I will rejoice in Jerusalem, and joy in my people: and the voice of weeping shall no more be heard in her, nor the voice of crying."

And then the prophet goes on to say, that they shall plant vineyards, and build houses, and do other things which are only appropriate to men in the flesh on earth. And all this is to occur when the wolf and the lamb shall feed together, and the lion eat straw like the bullock.

The new heavens and the new earth, then, according to Isaiah, consists in the restoration of Jerusalem, and in the removal of all weeping and sorrow from the earth, and in the production of just that restoration of all things in our world, of which God's holy prophets have so generally spoken, and which manifestly constitutes the millennium.

But let it be borne in mind that Isaiah and Peter speak of the same new heavens and new earth: for the apostle says, that his are the fulfilment of those predicted by the prophet. "We, according to his promise," that is, this promise of Isaiah, "look for a new heavens and a new earth in which dwelleth righteousness."

But Peter declares that his are after the coming of the Lord, and the dissolving of the elements, and the burning of the earth; and Isaiah teaches that his are before or at the commencement of a state of things which can only take place during the restoration of Israel and a converted world: therefore, from a comparison of these scriptures, it is clear that the coming of the Lord must be before the conversion of the world or millennium. For as Peter places the new heavens and the new earth after the coming of the Lord, and Isaiah places them before a converted world, is it not certain that the coming of Christ must be pre-millennial? The conclusion cannot be avoided, unless it is disproved that Isaiah and Peter refer to the same new heavens and earth. But this cannot be:

for Peter declares, that he looked for the accomplishment of Isaiah's prediction or promise after the conflagration.

The same conclusion is reached by a comparison of 1 Corinthians 15 : 54, with Isaiah 25 : 6-9.

In this chapter, the apostle argues extendedly concerning the resurrection of the dead. And then, when the dead are raised, and the living changed to immortal, he says, "So when this corruption shall have put on incorruption, and this mortal shall have put on immortality, then shall be brought to pass the saying that is written, Death is swallowed up in victory."

It will not be doubted by any that all this takes place after the second glorious appearance of our Lord. But mark, this result is the fulfilment of a prophecy, "Then shall be brought to pass, or fulfilled, the saying that is written, Death is swallowed up in victory."

Now, this saying is found in Isaiah 25 : 6-9. Let us read it, and see when it is to be accomplished, according to the prophet. "And in this mountain shall the Lord of Hosts make unto all people a feast of fat things, a feast of wines on the lees, of fat things full of marrow, of wines on the lees well refined. And he will destroy in this mountain the face of the covering cast over all people, and the veil that is spread over all nations. He will swallow up death in victory; and the Lord God will wipe away tears from off all faces; and the rebuke of his people shall he take away from off all the earth; for the Lord hath spoken it. And it shall be said in that day, Lo, this is our God, we have waited for him, and he will save us: this is the Lord; we have waited for him, we will be glad and rejoice in his salvation.

Now the prophet manifestly describes a state of things which is to come to pass here in our world—a latter day glory, in which great prosperity, holiness, and happiness are to reign—a converted, a restored world—the millennium, in which *death* is to be swallowed up in victory, and consequently a world in which tears shall be wiped away from all faces, and the rebuke of God removed from off all the earth.

This great, sublime, and glorious result, of which Isaiah speaks, is evidently to take place here on earth, and during the progress of the period represented. But the apostle says, it is to be brought to pass after the coming of Christ, and at the resurrection of the dead in Christ; therefore, the conclusion is unavoidable, that the coming of our Lord must be before the millennium: for as the apostle places it after the coming of the Lord, and Isaiah places it before or during the progress of a restored world, there is no other way in which their statements can be harmonized, but by the pre-millennial advent of our Lord and Saviour. And on this view of the subject they do harmonize most consistently and beautifully. But

8. It is manifest that the second coming of Christ is before the conversion of the world, from the consideration, that in the New Testament we are continually exhorted to look for, and be ready for the coming, or glorious appearing of the Lord Jesus Christ, as the great and grand event in which the hopes of the Christian and the world centre.

It would occupy more space than is desired, to refer to all the passages in which the second coming of our Lord is presented, as an object of hope, and a motive to obedience, in every good word and work; and especially as it is proposed to present them in another place, to show the practical bearings of the system, they will for the most part be omitted here. A few quotations only will be made.

Titus 2 : 11. "For the grace of God which bringeth salvation, hath appeared to all men, teaching us, that denying ungodliness and worldly lusts, we should live soberly, righteously, and godly, in this present world; looking for that blessed hope, and the *glorious appearing* of the great God, our Saviour Jesus Christ."

This certainly teaches that our eye is to be continually fixed upon the appearing of Christ, as our blessed hope.

Phil. 3 : 20. "For our conversation is in heaven; from whence also we look for the Saviour, the Lord Jesus Christ, who shall change our vile bodies, that they may be fashioned like unto his glorious body."

1 Pet. 4 : 12. "Beloved think it not strange concerning the fiery trial which is to try you, as though some strange thing happened unto you; but rejoice, inasmuch as ye are partakers of Christ's sufferings; that *when* his glory shall be revealed, ye may be glad also with exceeding joy."

1 Pet. 1 : 13. "Gird up the loins of your mind, be sober and hope to the end for the grace that is to be brought unto you *at the* revelation of Jesus Christ."

2 Tim 4 : 1. "I charge thee, therefore, before God, and the Lord Jesus Christ, who shall judge the quick, and the dead, *at his appearing*, and kingdom."

These are only a specimen of the very numerous passages which point us directly and steadily to the coming of Christ, as the great event in which all scriptural hopes centre. And they are to the point in showing, that no such thing as a millennium or a converted world is to be expected before He comes: for if all that the prophets have foretold, respecting the redemption of our world, is to be fulfilled before the second advent, why did our Lord and his apostles overlook and overleap all such events, and continually direct us to His appearing, for the consummation of all our hopes?

Their teachings and exhortations are certainly in striking harmony with the millennarian expectations.

Well then, as the scriptures teach that this world is to be converted, and perfectly restored to sinlessness and immortality, and yet never teach that it is to take place before His second advent, but admonish us to be continually looking for His coming, the conclusion seems to be unavoidable, that the restitution of all things must be after his advent, when he shall come a second time, without sin unto salvation; that is, when he comes again, he will not come to offer Himself a sacrifice for sin, but He will come in triumph, as a glorious Prince, to perfect and give universal success to his salvation over the world.

Before closing the argument for the pre-millennial advent of our Lord, it will be proper to notice some prominent objections which are generally and frequently urged, as triumphant refutations of all that can be said in its favor.

1. It is objected that the coming of Christ cannot be before the millennium—because the scriptures teach that the Son of Man will not come until he comes to judgment at the last day.

But it is in strict accordance with millennarian views, that Christ will judge the quick and the dead at his appearing and kingdom. The discussion of the judgment cannot be introduced here, without anticipating what will be the theme of another chapter. If the reader, therefore, will bear a little, it will be shown, that not a particle of all that the scriptures teach respecting the judgment of the righteous and the wicked, and of the time when it will occur, is denied by the views presented.

2. It is objected to the personal reign of Christ on earth, in a gloriously manifested kingdom, that it is contradicted by the declaration of the Lord himself, before Pilate, John 18: 36, when he said, "My kingdom is not of this world; if my kingdom were of this world, then would my servants fight, that I should not be delivered to the Jews; but now is my kingdom not from hence."

But what did the Saviour mean by this? Did he mean that his kingdom, which he came into this world to set up, was not, or would not be in this world? that it would never here in any sense be manifested? Or did he not rather mean, that his kingdom was not of this world, in the sense that others are, which are sustained by war, injustice, oppression and misrule?

It is manifest that the kingdom over which Christ shall reign, in the new dispensation, cannot be of or from this world from various considerations. And—

1. It will not be of or from this world, because he will receive it—not from the world, but from God, as the purchase of his death.

2. It will be a kingdom set up, not by human authority, power, or choice; but directly by Divine appointment; for, "In those days shall the God of heaven set up a kingdom, which shall never be destroyed."—Daniel 2: 44. It is hence clearly not of this world.

3. It is not a kingdom of or from this world, in the sense that other kingdoms are, in that it will be governed, not by human laws, not by worldly principles or policy, but by the laws of heaven, and the principles of eternal rectitude and love. It will be a theocracy, a government, or kingdom of God, and hence in no common sense of or from this world.

4. The kingdom of Christ is not of this world, in the same sense that he says of his disciples, John 17: 16, "They are not of the world, even as I am not of the world."

But in what sense were the apostles not of the world? were they so spiritual that they could not be seen? so mysteriously internal that they were no longer in or upon the world as a place of living and acting?

But though the apostles were not of the world, were not devoted to worldly interests and pursuits in opposition to Christ, yet they were personally in this world. This was the place of their abode, and of their labors and trials.

Just so, Christ's kingdom is not of this world; but yet it

is a kingdom in this world, and not in some other. It is for a kingdom in this world that we are taught to pray, "Thy kingdom come, Thy will be done on earth as it is in heaven." And it is out of this kingdom, here in this world, that the tares are to be gathered, and in which the righteous are to shine forth as the sun.

This declaration, therefore, of our Lord before Pilate, does not at all conflict with the idea of a visibly and gloriously manifested theocracy, or kingdom of God on earth.

The prophet Daniel clearly and incontrovertibly teaches that the kingdom of the God of heaven is to have a visible manifestation, and a subduing power on earth. In the second chapter of his prophesy, in interpreting the dream of Nebuchadnezzar respecting the great image, he says, "that the image, in its various parts, symbolized a succession of kingdoms which would arise in the world, from his time, down to the setting up of another kingdom by the God of heaven. This kingdom is represented by the little stone cut out of the mountain without hands, which smote the image upon the feet, and broke them to pieces. "Then was the iron, the clay, the brass, the silver, and the gold, broken to pieces together, and became like the chaff of the summer-threshing floors; and the wind carried them away, that no place was found for them: and the stone that smote the image became a great mountain, and filled the whole earth."

The kingdom represented by this little stone, which smote the image, is thus explained by the prophet.

"And in the days of these kings shall the God of heaven set up a kingdom, which shall never be destroyed; and the kingdom shall not be left to other people, but it shall break in pieces and consume all these kingdoms, represented in the image, and it shall stand forever."

Now it cannot be disputed that all the kingdoms, symbolized in this image, the Babylonian, the Medo-Persian, the

Macedonian, the Roman, and those which arose upon the breaking up of the empire, were literal and temporal kingdoms here on earth. Must not, then, that other kingdom which the God of heaven will set up, which comes in their place, and which is to stand forever, and by which they are all to be broken in pieces and consumed, and driven away as the chaff, so that no place is found for them, be a literal and visible kingdom also? Does not the fact, that it destroys in its growth all these kingdoms, and fills their place, prove that it must have a real, visible, and glorious manifestation on earth, through eternal ages, after its establishment?

The same great truth is clearly implied in all those predictions which teach, "That the kingdoms of this world are to become the kingdoms of our Lord." So that, although the kingdom of Christ is not of this world, in any such sense as oppressive and worldly governments generally are, yet it is in this world, and will here have a career of visible and everlasting glory.

3. It is objected to the personal and visible reign of Christ on earth, that he said, when he was demanded of the Pharisees, "*when the* kingdom of God should come," Luke 17: 20, "The kingdom of God cometh not with observation, neither shall they say, lo, here! or lo, there! for behold the kingdom of God is within you."

From this it is argued, that the kingdom of God is a purely spiritual kingdom, existing only in the hearts of men, and is therefore something which cannot be seen by outward observation.

But is this, or anything like it, the reason our Lord assigns why it will not come with observation?

The verses immediately succeeding show in what sense he meant to be understood; but he does not intimate that the reason is because his kingdom is so spiritual. He says it will not come with observation, because it will come so suddenly and unexpectedly. It will be as the lightning's flash, as it was with the flood in the days of Noah, and as the descent of fire on Sodom in the days of Lot. "And they shall say to you, see here! see there! Go not after them, nor follow them. For as the lightning that lighteneth out of one part under heaven, shineth unto the other part under heaven, so shall also the Son of Man be in his day. And as it was in the days of Noah, so shall it be also in the days of the Son of man. They did eat, they drank, they married wives, they were given in marriage, until the day that Noah entered into the ark, and the flood came and destroyed them all."

Likewise also as it was in the days of Lot: "they did eat, they drank, they bought, they sold, they planted, they builded; But the same day that Lot went out of Sodom, it rained fire and brimstone from heaven, and destroyed them all: Even thus shall it be in the day when the Son of Man is revealed."

The idea here presented is, that when the Son of Man is revealed in his kingdom, it will be so sudden, and unattended by any premonitory signs, that it will in no sense come with observation. The whole course of nature will remain unchanged and move on as usual. Iniquity will abound, and the love of many will wax cold. Scoffers will arise, and on every hand turn up the lip at those who are anxiously looking for that blessed hope, and the glorious appearing of the great God our Saviour; and exultingly exclaim, "Where is the promise of his coming: for since the fathers fell asleep all things continue as they were from the foundation of the world?"

In public and private life, all will be busy, as in times past, in their schemes of selfishness, and pride, and pleasures. Kings upon their thrones, or in secret conclave assembled, will be consulting how their power and tyranny may be perpetuated; and around them the sea and waves of popular discontent and commotion will be roaring, perhaps with unwonted restlessness.

There will be marrying and giving in marriage, buying and selling, building and planting, cheating and robbing, sickening, and suffering, and dying; just as it was on the day that Noah entered into the ark. Wickedness, as then, great, perilous, and heaven-daring will abound; and in the church, the wise and foolish virgins will be sleeping and slumbering together, over the coming of the bridegroom. False prophets and errorists of various names and pretensions will arise, and in putting forth their claims cry, lo, here! or lo, there! see here! or see there! and will delude many.

But suddenly at some unexpected moment, the Lord will descend from heaven with a shout, with the voice of the archangel, and the trump of God, and on every hand the cry will be heard, "Behold, the bridegroom cometh, Go ye out to meet him!" Oh what a cry will that be in the ears of an ungodly and slumbering world! "And then will be seen the sign of the Son of Man coming in the clouds of heaven, with power and great glory; and every eye shall see him, and they also which pierced him, and all the kindreds of the earth shall wail because of him."

Surely the kingdom of God will not come with observation. It will be as when the lightning flashes; we cannot say, see there! it comes; but, it is here. It has come in all its glory.

No one in respect to this kingdom, which will come at the appearing of Jesus Christ, can say, Lo, here! or Lo, there! which might be the case, were it such a kingdom as Spiritualists expect—a gradual development of the means in progress, until all shall ripen by slow progression "into the noon-tide glories of the millennial day!"

Then it might be said, see here, this revival! see yonder, the evangelization of an island! Lo, there, idolatry tottering!

or, Lo, here, a whole nation converted! See what progress is made; what light breaks forth on the darkness of ages, and how the signs of the times indicate the coming and triumph of the kingdom of our Lord! Were this progress of the gospel all that is meant by the kingdom of Christ, it would indeed come with observation; but as it is to come at the appearing of Jesus Christ, and this to be, for suddenness, as the lightning's flash, it will not come with observation. And this is in accordance with the Saviour's own exposition, and is in exact harmony with the millennarian's expectation.

When the Saviour said, in this connection, to the inquiring and hypocritical Pharisees, who demanded of him, *when* the kingdom of God should appear, "the kingdom of God is within you," He could not have meant that it was in their corrupt hearts. He must have meant simply, that the kingdom of God was among them, as our Lord declared in Luke 10 : 11:—"Be ye sure of this, that the kingdom of God is come nigh unto you." It was offered to them. They might have accepted the offered gospel, and thus have become heirs of the kingdom, which is to be manifested at the appearing of Christ.

4. It is frequently asserted that the personal reign of Christ, over a gloriously manifested kingdom on earth, is, or will be opposed to his spiritual reign. But how so? When Christ comes to be admired in all them that believe, will they admire him less on account of his presence? Does his personal presence and glory in heaven interfere with his spiritual rule in their souls by faith and love?

Shall we love the Saviour less when we see him as he is; and will his laws and spirit have a less potent influence in bringing every thought, and feeling, and desire into conformity to his will? As we view the subject, the personal presence and manifested glory of the Redeemer, will be vastly promotive of his spiritual reign, and give to it an efficacy which has never yet been witnessed on earth. It will be the establishment of heaven's spiritual rule in this revolted world, and will give it here an everlasting and indisputable supremacy.

5. It has been thought derogatory to the infinite glory and exalted dignity of the Saviour, that he should leave the heaven of heavens, to fix his throne as a monarch on earth, to preside in a city, and reign over this insignificant planet. It is said, "The period of our Lord's humiliation is past. Now he is seated on the throne of glory in the heavens. Shall he leave that throne to preside in a city, or reign even over the whole earth as a kingdom?"

"But Millennarians, if we understand their views, do not suppose that when the kingdom of God shall come on earth, that it will be confined to it, or be limited in its duration to a thousand years. Nor do they suppose, the Lord Jesus Christ, the appointed heir of all things, who has ascended far above all heavens, that he may fill all things, will, during that period, confine his presence to earth, or his dominion to the sons of Adam. They do suppose, however, that at the epoch in question, the kingdom, and dominion, and greatness of the kingdom under the whole heaven, will be added to his already immeasurably vast dominions. The accession of the Lord Jesus Christ, at his second coming, to this new kingdom, over which Satan has so long reigned, will not be the relinquishment of his natural or hereditary kingdon as the Son of God; nor of his mediatorial kingdom as the Son of Man. It will be no new humiliation; but a triumph over Satan, sin, and the curse, and the restoration of a lost world to its proper place in the creation of God."

Cowper conceived more justly of the object of the Saviour's advent in his kingdom, in the following lines:

"Come then, and added to thy many crowns
Receive yet one, the crown of all the earth,

Thou who alone art worthy! Thine it was
By ancient covenant ere nature's birth,
And thou hast made it thine by purchase since,
And overpaid its value by thy blood!
Come, then, and added to thy many crowns,
Receive yet one, as radiant as the rest,
Due to thy last and most effectual works,
Thy word fulfilled, the conquest of a world."

Other difficulties and objections to Messiah's reign on earth will be considered in subsequent chapters, and perhaps in some of these the reader may find the one which obstructs his own understanding and reception of the views presented.

In the scriptures which have been presented to prove the universal restoration of all things in our world, and the universal reign of Christ, it could hardly have escaped the notice of any, that they uniformly assert, in a variety of forms, that the kingdom which is to be here established, is to be an everlasting kingdom, and is to exist absolutely without end.

This, it is true, is contrary to a very common opinion held among men, that the kingdom of Christ *on earth* is at some future time to come to an end, and the world to be burned up and destroyed. But let God be true, though every man is made a liar.

Daniel says, 2 : 44, "And in the days of those kings shall the God of heaven set up a kingdom, *which shall never be destroyed :* and the kingdom shall not be left to other people, but it shall break in pieces and consume all these kingdoms, *and it shall stand forever.*" So in chapter 7 : 27, he says, "Whose kingdom is an *everlasting* kingdom, and all dominions shall serve and obey him."

Rev. 11 : 15. "And the seventh angel sounded; and there were great voices in heaven, saying : The kingdoms of this world are become the kingdoms of our Lord and of his Christ; *and he shall reign forever and ever.*"

The angel Gabriel said to Mary, Luke 1 : 32, 33, "He shall be great, and shall be called the Son of the Highest; and the Lord God shall give unto him the throne of his father David. *And he shall reign over the house of Jacob for ever*, and *of his kingdom there shall be no end.*" Does not this language preclude the possibility of limitation? There is to be no end to that government which he is to exercise over the house of Jacob in this world.

Psalms 72 : 5–8. "They shall fear thee as long as the sun and the moon endure, throughout all generations: He shall come down like rain upon the mown grass; as showers that water the earth. In his days shall the righteous flourish: and abundance of peace so long as the moon endureth. He shall have dominion, also, from sea to sea, and from the river unto the end of the earth." 2 : 11–17. "Yea, all kings shall fall down before him; all nations shall serve him. His name shall endure forever; his name shall be continued as long as the sun, and men shall be blessed in him; all nations shall call him blessed."

In these passages, it is not only declared that his kingdom on earth shall endure forever, but shall exist as long as the sun and the moon. Now, if, as will be shown in a subsequent chapter, there is no such thing predicted in scripture as the annihilation of these heavenly bodies, or of earth, it will follow that our world will be inhabited forever, and that during eternal ages Christ will rule over it.

Isaiah says, 9 : 7, "*Of the increase* of his government and peace there shall be *no end*, upon the throne of David, and upon his kingdom to order it, and to establish it with judgment and with justice, *from henceforth, even forever.*"

Let it be supposed, that after sin, and the curse, and all the works of the devil are destroyed from earth, the generations of sanctified men in the flesh shall go on increasing, eternally, and that as they fulfill their lot in life, they shall, to make room for others, be transfigured to the glorified, without tasting death, as were Enoch and Elijah, how literally and sublimely would this prediction of Isaiah be fulfilled. "Of the increase of his government there would indeed then be no end." And as the redeemed passed away from earth, there would be room enough for them amid the bright orbs above, or in those mansions in our Father's house which Jesus has gone to prepare.

How this simple and scriptural view magnifies the salvation of Jesus! how it enhances the triumphs of Divine love! what a sublime spectacle will be a redeemed world for the universe to look upon through unending ages; and as the holy thus continue to increase, how will the number of the lost continue to diminish in comparison, until they shall be only as the drop to the ocean to the saved. Then, indeed, will the Crucified see of the travail of his soul and be satisfied. Then, indeed, will the trophies of grace as far exceed the utmost stretch of human conception, as this mighty universe does our limited vision. If these scriptures do not prove the everlasting duration of Christ's kingdom on earth, then it would be impossible to prove the eternity of God, or the eternity of future happiness, or misery, from the Word of God; for on the same principles by which any would explain these scriptures to represent only a limited time, others of the same kind, referring to the future world, might be limited. How much more safe to take the scriptures according to their literal and obvious import.

And now may I not ask, why should it be thought a thing incredible, or unreasonable, that he who so loved the world, as once to live in it, and to die for it, should again descend in mercy to perfect that work, which, from the foundation of the world, he commenced and loved—to subdue all things to himself, and here to multiply his seed through everlasting ages, freed from sin and the curse, until their numbers shall outswell the sands of the sea-shore, and exceed the stars of heaven for multitude and glory? Can any say that this would be unworthy of the love of God, or degrading to his infinite dignity and power? Sublime and beautiful, and glorious as is this vast scheme of redeeming love, we would not dare receive it did it not appear to be clearly predicted in the scriptures of truth; but believing it here revealed, and seeing its entire harmony with all the other recorded doctrines of scripture, we accept it as scriptural, rational, and infinitely worthy of God.

"Come, thou Desire of nations, quickly come!
Conqueror of death, break up the gloomy tomb;
Star of thine Israel, call the wanderers in;
Healer of Nature's wounds, thy work begin;
Thou nearest Kinsman, come, avenge our wrongs,
Our sorrows turn to joy, our sighs to songs."

Chapter Fifth.

THE RESURRECTION, TRANSFIGURATION, AND REIGN OF THE SAINTS.

WITH the glorious appearing of our Lord and Saviour Jesus Christ to reign upon the earth, are associated various events of great significance and grandeur. Among these, first in the order of time and importance are the resurrection of the dead and transfiguration of the living saints, and their adjudgment to thrones and crowns in his kingdom.

"For if we believe that Jesus died, and rose again, even so them also which sleep in Jesus will God bring with him. For the Lord himself shall descend from heaven with a shout, with the voice of the archangel, and with the trump of God: and the dead in Christ shall rise first: Then we which are alive and remain shall be caught up together with them in the clouds, to meet the Lord in the air; and so shall we ever be with the Lord. Wherefore comfort one another with these words."—1 Thess. 4: 14–18.

According to millennarian understanding of the scriptures, there are to be two resurrections of the dead widely separated from each other in time and portentous significance. In proof of this, the passage in Revelations 20: 1–7, will first be considered.

"And I saw an angel come down from heaven, having the key of the bottomless pit and a great chain in his hand. And he laid hold on the dragon, that old serpent, which is the devil and satan, and bound him a thousand years, and cast him into the bottomless pit, and shut him up, and set a seal upon him, that he should deceive the nations no more, till the thousand years should be fulfilled; and after that he must be loosed a little season.

"And I saw thrones, and they sat upon them, and judgment was given unto them; and I saw the souls of them that were beheaded for the witness of Jesus, and for the word of God, and which had not worshipped the beast, neither his image, neither had received his mark upon their foreheads, or in their hands, and they lived and reigned with Christ a thousand years. But the rest of the dead lived not again until the thousand years were finished. This is the first resurrection. Blessed and holy is he that hath part in the first resurrection: on such the second death hath no power, but they shall be priests of God and of Christ, and shall reign with him a thousand years. And when the thousand years are expired, Satan shall be loosed out of his prison," &c.

The import of this passage seems to be very plain. Most who are not millennarians, as well as those who are, have understood it to teach that Satan is to be banished from the earth, and effectually restrained from all evil influence in our world during the period of time here designated.

In this all adopt the most obvious sense; and following the same natural import, I see not how the conclusion can be avoided, that there are to be two resurrections, the one preceding, and the other following the thousand years. Of all who followed the Lamb, mentioned in chapter 19: 14, and who had not worshipped the beast, neither his image, it is said, "And they lived and reigned with Christ a thousand years. But the rest of the dead lived not again, [or were not raised as to their bodies from the dead] till the thousand years were finished. This is the first resurrection."

It is clear that the two resurrections here named must correspond to each other. If the first is a merely spiritual resurrection, meaning a resurrection from sin to holiness, then the second must be spiritual in the same sense, and would show that those raised at the close of the thousand years were to be also raised to holiness and happiness; but if either one is a literal resurrection of the dead, then consistency and common sense require that the other should be understood in the same sense. There is nothing in the passage to warrant us in saying that the first resurrection is spiritual, and that the second is a literal rising of the dead.

But it is rendered certain that there is a literal resurrection of the dead spoken of at the close of the thousand years: for the apostle immediately adds, verses 12, 13, "And I saw the dead, small and great, stand before God. And the sea gave up the dead which were in it; and death and hell delivered up the dead which were in them: and they were judged, every man according to their works. And death and hell were cast into the lake of fire. This is the second death.

Here, then, is evidence conclusive that the resurrection at the close of the thousand years, is a literal resurrection of the dead. And in addition to this, it is rendered certain that it is in no sense a spiritual resurrection spoken of: for upon them the second death does have power, which could not be the case were their resurrection one from sin to holiness; and they are pronounced neither blessed nor holy, neither do they reign with Christ.

From the necessity of the case, then, one resurrection is here clearly defined to denote a literal resurrection of the dead, which must consequently determine the nature of the other, and shows it is a literal resurrection of the dead in Christ. The vast difference made between the destinies of the two classes of persons here represented, cannot comport with the idea of a spiritual resurrection in each case, but is perfectly consistent with a literal resurrection of the bodies of the righteous and the wicked, as taught throughout the Scriptures. For there is nothing incongruous, absurd, or impossible in the idea that the holy should be raised before the thousand years, judged and rewarded with offices of glory in Christ's kingdom, and that when the thousand years are finished, the unholy should be raised and punished.

This exposition is sustained and argued by Professor Stuart, and others equally learned, as necessarily required by the very structure of the passage and the import of the words employed. Though most decidedly opposed to millennarian views, he maintains that, according to a correct exegesis of this passage, there must, and certainly will be a resurrection before the millennium. The words will not consistently and rationally bear any other construction. See Com. on Apoc., vol. I. p. 357.

In arriving at the conclusion, therefore, that two resurrections are here taught, and that the saints are to be raised before the millennium, we indulge in no vain speculations or imaginations. The meaning which lies on the very face of the passage is taken, that which is most obvious and clear, and which we believe God intended to communicate. And this conviction is strengthened from the consideration that neither the Saviour nor his apostles ever taught anything contrary to it, but much that is most strikingly and clearly in harmony with it. In fact, there are some scriptures which would have little or no force, except on the ground of the two resurrections here maintained.

In 1 Corinthians, chapter 15, the apostle Paul has presented an extended argument to prove the resurrection of the dead. He says, in verse 22 and onward, "For as in Adam all die, even so in Christ shall all be made alive. But every man in his own order: Christ the first fruits, afterwards *they that are Christ's* at his coming." There is great emphasis and distinctive meaning in these words, and they undoubtedly imply that the wicked, or those who are not Christ's, will not be raised at the same time. For where would be the force or propriety in saying that they who are Christ's are to be raised *at his coming*, if all who are not his are to be raised at the same period ?

Though all are at some time to rise and appear before the judgment seat of Christ, the just and the unjust, yet there is to be an orderly succession in these resurrections, and one, too, which will appropriately accord with the widely different destinies of the righteous and the wicked.

There is also a passage in Philippians 3: 8–12, which is in striking harmony with these views, and upon which they shed a clear and glorious light.

"But what things were gain to me, those I counted loss for Christ. Yea, doubtless, and I count all things but loss for the excellency of the knowledge of Christ Jesus my Lord: for whom I have suffered the loss of all things, and do count them but dung, that I may win Christ, and be found in him, not having mine own righteousness, which is of the law, but that which is through the faith of Christ, the righteousness which is of God by faith. That I may know him, and the power of his resurrection, and the fellowship of his sufferings, being made conformable unto his death ; *if by any means I might attain unto the resurrection of the dead.* Not as though I had already attained ; but I follow after, if that I may apprehend that for which also I am apprehended of Christ Jesus."

Let it be noticed, that the apostle declares that he suffered the loss of all things, and made all the effort he here describes. "If by any means he might attain unto the resurrection of the dead," and that this was the work for which he pressed.

Now what does this mean ? What resurrection was this,

to which Paul was so anxious to attain, and for which he sacrificed so much? It cannot refer to a spiritual resurrection, for to this he had already attained by being born of the spirit, when he was made a new creature in Christ Jesus.

Nor can it consistently refer to a resurrection promiscuously of the righteous and the wicked: for to this he could not help attaining, let him do what he might. God has purposed and revealed that all who are in their graves shall hear the voice of the Son of God and come forth. It was not necessary, therefore, that the apostle, or others, should make any effort to secure this. But to the resurrection, of which he here speaks, there was a possibility of his not attaining. To attain it, required all the self-denial and effort enjoined in the gospel. What then can it mean?

Behold, how simply and forcibly it harmonizes with the doctrine of two resurrections, as set forth. On the ground that there are to be two resurrections, the one widely separated from the other in time, nature, and glory, and that "Blessed and holy is he that hath part in the first resurrection, for on such the second death hath no power," and that all such are to be kings and priests unto God, it is not wonderful that the apostle was anxious to attain to it; and it may readily be seen why effort and holiness are necessary to participate in it.

O, who would not, did he believe in such a resurrection, commend the apostle, and strive with him in equally ardent and self denying effort to gain so great and glorious a prize? How many will never be counted worthy to attain this resurrection of the just, and will be shut out from all its glories into outer darkness, to come forth only to the resurrection of condemnation: because they never sought, or lived for it. Reader, are you striving, like the great apostle, that you may attain unto the resurrection of the dead?

This seems to have been the prize, too, for which the ancient worthies contended. Of all those who died in the faith, Paul says, Heb. 11: 35, "And others were tortured, not accepting deliverance, that they might attain a better resurrection." What resurrection? Manifestly not the general; for this they could not avoid, however wicked. Not a spiritual; for this they had already experienced, before they left the world. Nor did they suffer what they did, merely that they might live hereafter; for this they could not avoid. But they were undoubtedly, like Paul, looking and living for this first resurrection, in which the righteous only will be concerned, and be blessed and holy.

According to this view, it needs no philosophizing or spiritualizing to understand these scriptures, and to give them a surpassing force and beauty.

The doctrine of a first resurrection, widely distinguished from that of a general one, in which all the wicked are included, receives additional proof and illustration from several passages in the teachings of our Saviour.

Luke, 14: 14. "But when thou makest a feast, call the poor, the maimed, the lame, the blind, and thou shalt be blessed: for they cannot recompense thee: for thou shalt be recompensed *at the resurrection of the just.*"

Does not this imply that the resurrection of the just will be something distinct from a general one, in which all will be included? A promiscuous resurrection, in which a large proportion, and perhaps a majority might be unholy, could not, with truth and propriety, be termed *the resurrection of the just.* And besides, the passage shows that the just are not to receive their peculiar reward in the kingdom of God, until the resurrection. It associates their recompense, as the scriptures uniformly do, with this great and glorious event.

Without doing any violence, therefore, to the passage, or laboring to twist it from its most obvious import, it certainly accords most perfectly with the doctrine of the two resurrections in question.

Another wonderful passage, difficult to understand on the ground of but one resurrection, promiscuous and universal, but entirely free from all obscurity in the light of the views presented, is found in Luke 20: 34–36:

"And Jesus answered, and said unto them, the children of this world marry and are given in marriage: But they, which shall be accounted worthy to attain that world, *and* the *resurrection from the dead,* neither marry, nor are given in marriage: neither can they die any more: for they are equal unto the angels; and are the children of God, being the children of the resurrection."

Now read this passage in the light of the two resurrections, the first or that of the just, possessing all the glory, and holiness, and blessedness ascribed to it in Revelations 20, and all is clear and beautiful.

When the just shall all be like Christ, and their vile bodies fashioned like unto his glorious body, at his appearing and kingdom, then it will appear, indeed, that they are the children of God, being the children of the *first* resurrection: for none will be counted worthy to obtain this world, or this resurrection, but the pure in heart. "Blessed and holy is he that hath part in the first resurrection: for on such the second death shall have no power."

But how would this passage read, or be explained, on the supposition that the wicked are to attain to the resurrection of the dead, at the same time, and in the same manner with the righteous?

The evidence is then conclusive, that there is to be a first resurrection, in which the just only will participate, and that this is separated in time from that of the wicked, by a period denoted by that of a thousand years.

And this conclusion is in no way weakened or set aside, by

those passages which declare, in general terms, that there will be a resurrection both of the just and the unjust, without determining the order in which, and the time when, they are to take place.

John 5: 28, 29. "Marvel not at this; for the hour is coming, in the which all that are in their graves shall hear the voice of the Son of God, and shall come forth; they that have done good unto the resurrection of life; and they that have done evil unto the resurrection of damnation."

This and similar passages speak of the resurrection in general terms, and undoubtedly include all classes of men who ever have died or shall die in time to come; but it is clear that they do not determine the times or the order of the resurrection.

Should the scriptures, in other connections, declare that the dead would be raised at two or twenty different times, and in as many different lands, separated each by a month or year, there would be no contradiction, for it would still be true that all would hear the voice of the Son of God, and come forth from their graves, though at different periods. So neither do those scriptures which teach that the just and unjust shall be raised up, in general terms, without fixing the time, contradict the plainly revealed fact, that those who are Christ's are to be raised up first, at his coming, and that the rest of the dead will not live again until the thousand years are ended.

But should it further be maintained that the resurrection of the righteous and the wicked, and all the scenes of the last and eternal judgment, together with the burning of the world, must necessarily take place at the same time, because they are all associated in scripture with the second coming of Christ—it is answered, that this does not follow as a consequence.

They will undoubtedly all take place at, or in association

with the second coming of our Lord. But what are we to understand by the coming of Christ? Does it denote an instant of time—the twinkling of an eye; or all the time, be it longer or shorter, which may be necessary for him to accomplish in orderly succession, all that he has said he will do? Does the coming of Christ represent simply the length of time which may be occupied in his descent from heaven to earth, or that moment when he may appear in mid heaven? And can we reasonably suppose that all the great events predicted to take place at that time, are to occur and be finished in that instant of time? Would it not be more consistently in accordance with these things, to conclude that by the coming of Christ is designated all that period of time which will be necessary to accomplish the work for which he comes?

At the day of judgment, we are assured that every individual, of all the vast millions of mankind, from Adam down, must give an account of himself to God, and that God will bring every work into judgment with every secret thing, whether it be good or bad. And this will be necessary, not to inform God, or to enable him to render in each case a right verdict, but that a created and intelligent universe may see that God is just, and understand the mystery of his proceedings.

And let none be startled at the length of time which this may occupy; for God has no need to be in a hurry. One day is with the Lord as a thousand years, and a thousand years as one day, and there will be time enough in advance to accomplish all that he has said he will do.

Now, as all these predicted events, in detail, are to take place at the coming of Christ, and as some length of time, unrevealed, must transpire in their accomplishment, it is certain that the second coming of our Lord must denote, not an instant, but a period of time long enough, at least, for the accomplishment of all his acts of judgment and salvation.

And hence the scriptural representations respecting the coming of Christ, and all the fearful solemnities of the judgment of the great day which cluster around his coming, do not conflict with the doctrine that when Christ comes, he will first raise the dead, and transfigure the living saints, and then, by reckoning with them, adjudge them to thrones and offices in his kingdom, and afterward, in orderly succession and at the time appointed, do all which he has declared shall be done at his appearing. This enlarged, consistent, and rational view of the coming of our Lord gives full scope for the full and ample accomplishment of all his predicted purposes, and harmonizes the various representations of scripture, as will yet be shown.

But when the just are raised immortal, incorruptible, and glorious, at the coming of Christ, and the living saints on earth transfigured into their glorified forms, and caught up to meet the Lord in the air, for the purpose of judgment and reward, they will be associated with him in the government of the kingdom then to be fully set up.

The proof of this is abundant. A part only will be presented. 2 Tim. 2: 12.—"If we suffer, we shall also reign with him."

Rev. 3: 21. "To him that overcometh will I grant to sit with me in my throne, even as I also overcome, and am set down with my Father in his throne." These passages, with others equally explicit, teach that those who suffer with Christ, and who overcome sin and the world in their adherence to his cause, will reign with him. There would be no definite meaning in these promises, were they not to reign over some place or persons.

But there is nothing said here of the time when, or the place where, or the persons over whom they are to reign.

They point, however, to the future, to some period beyond the present, when in the faithfulness of God all shall be fulfilled.

If we turn now to Rev. 20: 4, we are definitely told of the time when they are to reign with him. "And they lived and reigned with Christ a thousand years," or during the millennium.

But nothing is said yet of the place where this reign is to be exercised or enjoyed. This point is settled by a reference to Rev. 5: 9, 10. "And they sung a new song, saying, Thou art worthy to take the Book, and to open the seals thereof: for thou wast slain, and hast redeemed us unto God by thy blood, out of every kindred, and tongue, and people, and nation; and hast made us unto our God kings and priests, *and we shall reign on the earth.*"

This is the song of the four living creatures, and the four-and-twenty elders, the symbolic representatives of the redeemed saints in heaven, heard in vision by John.

They praise the Lamb for his redeeming blood, for his exalted mercy in making them kings and priests unto God, and for that kingdom to which they are heirs, but of which they are not yet put in possession. Their language is peculiar. They do not say, we now reign before the throne; or, we shall reign hereafter in heaven; but, we shall reign upon the earth.

Now, what do all these scriptures teach, if it is not that the saints, the redeemed now in heaven, or who shall be there previous to the first resurrection, are to descend with the Lord, when he comes, and in their raised and glorified bodies to reign over men upon the earth?

Could language be more definite in affirming, that during the millennium, "The kingdom, and the greatness of the kingdom under the whole heaven, shall be given to the people of the saints." "Know ye not," says the apostle, "that the saints shall judge the world," or rule over it?

With this view of the subject accords most fully and beautifully the description given of the New Jerusalem, in its descent from God out of heaven to our earth: Rev. 21 and 22.

The New Jerusalem is not manifestly a literal, material city as some have vainly supposed; nor is it a representation of heaven, that glorious abode of God, where the spirits of just men made perfect are now assembled: for it is said to come down from God out of heaven to our earth, which shows that it is something entirely distinct and separate from heaven as a place or a state of blessedness. It would seem from the description given, that there is no room left for doubt or mistake in regard to its true scriptural import. "And there came unto me one of the seven angels, saying, Come hither, I will show thee the bride, the Lamb's wife. And he carried me away in the spirit to a great and high mountain, and showed me that great city, the holy Jerusalem, descending out of heaven from God."—Rev. 21: 9, 10.

Here, then, is one point definitely settled, that the new Jerusalem is the bride, the Lamb's wife, descending with him from heaven, prepared and adorned for her husband.

But who constitute the bride? Let us turn a little back in the same discourse, and see if any information is given.

Rev. 19: 6, 8. "And I heard as it were the voice of a great multitude, and as the voice of many waters, and as the voice of mighty thunderings, saying, Alleluia: for the Lord God Omnipotent reigneth. Let us be glad and rejoice, and give honor to him: for the marriage of the Lamb is come, and his wife hath made herself ready. And to her it was granted that she should be arrayed in fine linen, clean and white: for the *fine linen is,*" or represents "the *righteousness* of the saints."

Now, as it was given to the bride to be clothed in fine linen, and this fine linen is the righteousness of the saints, then it is here settled certainly and definitely that the saints —the congregated assembly of glorified spirits, constitute the bride, the Lamb's wife. And this is in accordance with the uniform representation of Scripture, and the common belief, that the church, composed of all the faithful and sanctified, is the spouse of Christ.

If, then, the saints are the bride of Christ, and the new Jerusalem is also his wife as declared, then the new Jerusalem must necessarily be regarded as a symbol or representative of the saints, the redeemed church—as they descend with him at his second coming. But what is meant by their marriage? The apostle Paul teaches that when the saints descend with Christ, their vile bodies are to be raised, and fashioned like unto his glorious body; and that then they are to receive their crowns of glory, and are to sit down with him in his throne, agreeably to promise.

Now what could so beautifully represent all this as a marriage? The saints are now united to him by faith and love; but the union is not perfect, and has not been publicly consummated. But when their vile bodies are raised and made like his, and when in association with him, they are publicly exalted to thrones and offices in his kingdom, then indeed will the marriage have come, and the union be perfected.

Accordingly, the whole description of the new Jerusalem in its association with the unglorified in the flesh, shows the influence and government which the saints are to exercise over the world.

The following extract is taken from Mr. Lord's work on the Apocalypse:—

"As the city is the symbol of the Lamb's wife, the raised and glorified saints adopted as joint heirs with Christ, exalted to thrones and associated with him in his reign on earth, its descent to earth symbolizes their descent from heaven after their justification, and investiture as kings and priests in his empire.

"The splendor of the elements of which it is built, denotes the beauty of their persons and the perfection of their character; its magnitude, immensely transcending the vastest extent over which the unaided eye can discern the most brilliant objects on the surface of the earth, denotes the incomprehensible greatness of their multitude; and the regularity of its form, the harmony of its parts, and its massiveness and strength, the symmetry of their relations to each other, the unity of their spirit, and the energy of their sway.

"The gates symbolize the access to the glorified which the nations are to enjoy. That there is to be no night there, signifies that they are never to be without the visible presence of God; that its gates are never shut, denotes that the nations are to enjoy uninterrupted access to the glorified.

"In the temple of Jerusalem, the mercy seat, the symbol of the throne of God in the scene of the visible displays of his presence, was in the holy of holies, wholly withdrawn from the sight of the worshippers, and beheld only by the high priest once a year. That there is no temple in the new Jerusalem, denotes, therefore, that the presence of the Redeemer is to be visible to the worshippers at large, not, as under the Mosaic dispensations, veiled from sight.

"As the sun and the moon are symbols of the supreme legislative and executive rulers in a state, that the city has no need of the sun nor the moon that they may enlighten it, for the glory of God enlightens it, and its lamp is the Lamb, denotes that it is to have no need that the unglorified or glorified saints should make laws for it, as God is to be its law-giver, and Christ to supply it with all the commands and counsels its exigencies are to require.

"That the nations are to walk by its light, signifies that they are to be guided by the teachings which Christ communicates to the glorified saints. That the kings of the earth bring their glory and honor into it, implies that the chiefs of the nations are to exercise their office in perfect subordination to the saints whom it symbolizes, and employ themselves in subserving the ends which they enjoin.

"That no one is to enter it that is unclean, or that works defilement, or falsehood, indicates that sanctification is requisite in order to that relation to the glorified which admission to its gates denotes, and thence as all nations are to walk in its light, that the race is universally to be holy.

"The river of the water of life, proceeding from the throne of God and of the Lamb, is the symbol, doubtless, of the renewing and sanctifying influences, by which the nations are to be imbued with spiritual life.

"The leaves of the tree of life, which are for the healing of the nations, symbolize the means of their restoration from mortality; and the fruit of that tree, the pledge of their transfiguration to glory; for *there shall* be no curse any more."

For a further illustration of the New Jerusalem, the reader is referred to the work from which this extract is made.

Now, whatever may be thought of the detailed application here made, it is clear, that as the New Jerusalem is the symbol, or representative of the saints, as they descend to the resurrection and marriage of the Lamb, there is indicated here a most intimate, joyous, and glorious intercourse between the raised and glorified saints, caught up with Christ into the air, and the unglorified nations in the flesh, over whom the saints under Christ, are to reign.

The New Jerusalem state, then, is in perfect harmony with the doctrine of a first resurrection, and the reign of the saints over a redeemed and restored world in a new dispensation

It cannot be a representation of that glorious place, in some part of the universe, called heaven, nor of a state of things existing there; for it descends from God out of heaven to our earth, and here the *nations* walk in its light, and kings bring their glory into it, and the leaves of the tree of life in the midst of it, are, not for the pure in heaven, not for the healing of any there, for none there need healing; but for the healing of the nations on earth. But how could you explain this New Jerusalem state, if you deny the reign of the saints, and refer it to heaven alone? Will heaven itself as a place descend to earth, and will there be nations there to be healed, and kings there to bring their glory, and to walk in its light?

For myself, I never understood anything of what was really meant by the descent of the New Jerusalem, and the glorious and happy intercourse between it and the nations of the earth, until the light and beauty of the millennial reign of the saints in a new dispensation dawned upon me.

But oh, how clear, and joyous, and consistent, with all the truths and revelations of God in his Word, does it now appear!

The scriptures, thus far presented, in proof of the reign of the saints on earth, are sustained by many others, upon which we cannot much enlarge in exposition.

Matt. 19: 28. " In the regeneration, when the Son of Man shall sit upon the throne of his glory, ye also shall sit upon twelve thrones judging the twelve tribes of Israel." What does this mean? How strikingly does it fall in with the view presented? In a regenerated world—the apostles raised and glorified, will be elevated to great honor and usefulness in the kingdom of Christ, in reigning over the converted and restored tribes of Israel. No one supposes that the apostles are to have twelve literal thrones built somewhere in Jerusalem or Palestine, upon which they are to sit. Their sitting upon thrones, simply represents their exaltation as princes over the restored tribes, just as the prophet Daniel represents the archangel, Michael, as one of their chief princes.

1. Corinthians 6: 2. "Know ye not that the saints shall judge the world? know ye not that the saints shall judge angels." How often has the question been asked, what do, or can these texts mean? Can they mean, that at the last great day, all the saints are to be associated with Christ in judging the secrets of all men according to his gospel, and in assigning them their eternal destinies? What! shall the saints be clothed with omniscience, and share in that awful work which, in every other part of scripture, is ascribed only to God?

But how simple and consistent these passages, when regarded only as declaring that the saints, under Christ, are yet to rule over the world, in a similar sense, probably, in which the angels now rule. And there is nothing absurd in the idea, that when Christ shall exalt his redeemed, and cause them, agreeably to his promise, to sit down with him in his throne, over this world, that some of the angels may not be as high as they, but subordinate, and that thus they may even judge or rule over angels.

Matt. 5: 5. "Blessed are the meek, for they shall inherit the earth." How often is this promise repeated in the prophetic scriptures; and yet, when have the meek, in any sense, inherited the earth? The meek now often have the least of this world, and are the most afflicted and tormented. Do they then inherit the earth? And as the promise points to the future, declaring that they shall inherit it, at some time to come, when will it be, if the saints are not yet to possess and reign over the world?

But when the meek of all ages, gathered now with the Saviour in heaven, shall descend with him, at the marriage of the Lamb, and be put in possession of the dominion of earth, how truly will all these promises be fulfilled, that the meek shall inherit the earth?

Isaiah 24 : 33. "Then the moon shall be confounded, and the sun ashamed," that is, the ruling powers of earth symbolized by the sun and moon, "when the Lord of hosts shall reign in Mount Zion, and in Jerusalem, and before his ancients, gloriously."

Zechariah, 14: 4, 6, 9. "And his feet shall stand, in that day, upon the Mount of Olives, which is before Jerusalem, on the east. And the Lord shall be king over all the earth: in that day shall there be one Lord, and his name one."

Job 19: 25–29. "For I know that my Redeemer liveth, and that I shall see him in the latter day *upon the earth:* and though after my skin, worms devour this body, yet in my flesh shall I see God: whom I shall see for myself, and mine eyes shall behold and not another; though my reins be consumed within me."

Did time permit, numerous other scriptures, and whole chapters might be quoted, which concentrate to this one point, and pour a flood of glorious effulgence over the future reign of Christ with his saints.

And, now, if the reader would form a correct estimate of millennarian views, and not pervert, or misrepresent them, he must bear in mind what has been repeatedly and distinctly referred to, that the raised and transfigured saints will be entirely distinct from the unglorified men and nations in the flesh. When the bodies of the dead saints are raised, and the living saints transfigured, they will be caught up together to meet the Lord in the air. This is according to express scripture. Beneath them, then, and separate from them, will be the earth with all the unglorified upon it, composed of unconverted Jews and Gentiles, and apostate Christendom.

All those who receive not the Saviour, and who will not that he should reign over them, will be destroyed from the earth, as were the inhabitants of the old world, and reserved with Sodom and Gomorrah, unto judgment at the resurrection of the wicked. All this will be proved and illustrated in a future chapter.

But the Jews will then receive the Redeemer, and will look on him whom they have pierced and mourn; and there will be remnants of all the Gentile nations, and probably whole heathen nations, who will receive him, and who by the wonderful outpourings of the spirit of God, will be converted. Let the reader take these points for granted, for the present, for the sake of illustration.

These unglorified Jews and Gentiles in the flesh, entirely distinct from the raised and glorified, will build houses, plant vineyards, and do all other things appropriate to men in the flesh, and which their worldly circumstances may require; and over these, Christ and his saints will reign.

All the prophetic promises, therefore, appropriate only to men in the flesh, will have no application to the raised and transfigured saints, but only to those living and multiplying on the earth as men do now.

Hence the imputation often made against millennarians, that they hold that the saints raised from the dead are to live right down here flat upon the earth, and be confined here, and jostle with men in the flesh, and live in houses, and multiply, is entirely untrue and out of character.

In the resurrection and transfigured state of the saints, they will be as distinct from men in the flesh, as the angels are from men now. And among them, there will be no marrying or giving in marriage, nor will their enjoyments consist in sensual pleasures, in any degrading, groveling, or unheavenly sense; for the kingdom of God, as we hold, will not be meats and drinks; but righteousness, peace, and joy in the Holy Ghost.

Nor do we suppose that the happiness of the unglorified in

that pure age, will consist in eating and drinking. Men will then not live to eat; but eat to live—eat to fulfil the end of their being, in accomplishing all the good purposes of their Lord.

Now, if any inquire how, or in what manner, the raised saints will mingle and associate with men, and exercise their government over them, we answer we do not certainly know.

But this does not disprove their reign, any more than does our inability to tell how, in all cases, the angels now minister to those who shall be heirs of salvation, disprove their ministry.

But if I may be allowed to express my own idea, I would draw an illustration from the angels.

You believe, Reader, that the angels are now all ministering spirits, sent forth to minister for those who shall be heirs of salvation—that the law was given on Sinai by the mediation of angels—that they continually encamp around them that fear the Lord—and that all along down through the history of the Divine administration, as revealed in scripture, they have been commissioned to do great and wonderful things—directing the pestilence and the storm, and executing the purposes of Jehovah in nature, providence, and grace.

Now suppose the veil was drawn aside, which conceals all these beings and things from mortal vision, and you were permitted to see these angels, as did the young man with the prophet Elisha, as they crowded the mountain around Samaria, as they encamp around the saints, and go forth in obedience to God, to fulfill their commissions of judgment or mercy, over all the earth; and, in my humble judgment, you would have an exhibition of the manner in which the saints, under Christ, will fulfill their offices. They will, doubtless, often hold personal, visible, and delightful intercourse with the unglorified in the flesh, as the angels did with Abraham, with Lot, and as Moses and Elisha did with Christ and Peter,

James and John, on the mount of transfiguration. But where in mid heavens, or amid the bright orbs above, they may spread forth their bright pavilions, when not in actual intercourse with the men on earth, is not revealed.

"It is often objected that the millennarian hypothesis robs the saints of the glories of heaven and sinks their joys to the level of sense. Their bodies it is said, will be spiritual and glorious, and they cannot belong to a material world. Now their spirits enjoy the beatific vision of God. They dwell in his presence, where is fulness of joy; shall they be degraded from their thrones of glory to the things of earth and sense?"

Millennarians are bound by their principles, to receive all these scriptures, in their full and perfect and literal sense, which describe the exalted, pure, and eternal blessedness of the righteous; and hence their views do not degrade or detract from the glory of the redeemed.

"To the question, which is often asked, how is it possible for numbers so vast as those which will compose the redeemed church, when raised from the dead, to find a resting place upon so inconsiderable a planet as this, Millennarians answer, they will not; nor do their views of the kingdom of God suppose they will. Being made like unto the angels, and equal unto the angels, they will not be confined to the earth by any necessity of their nature. The heavens, the whole realm of Christ, as the Son of Man, will be open to them. Being heirs of God, and conformed to the body of the glory of Jesus, and one with him, they will be with him wherever he is, beholding his glory, and executing, as the messengers of his power, his high behests throughout the kingdom of God.

"It is a misconception, therefore, to suppose that the glorified saints will leave the heavens, and mingle and jostle with men in the flesh, and share in their various occupations, as if they were subject to the same necessities of food, raiment, or shelter. Yet they do believe the glorified saints will have intercourse, perhaps frequent and intimate intercourse, with the inhabitants of the earth, although the manner of it they are unable to explain."

"If the spiritualist demands explicitness upon this point, and many others which may be stated, touching the expected economy, the millennarian inquires in his turn of the spiritualist, How could Moses and Elias appear to the disciples Peter, James, and John, on the holy mount? How could they join in conversation with the Lord Jesus Christ, both audibly and intelligibly to the disciples? How did they so suddenly disappear from their view?

"The power of God, which raised up Jesus from the dead, showed him openly from time to time during forty days, not to all the disciples, but to chosen witnesses. Where was he during the intervals of apparition? What was the manner of his being as a man? Could he be seen by others? He appeared and disappeared, in a manner quite unaccountable to the disciples—suddenly standing among them and joining in their conversation, and then vanishing out of their sight."

"These examples, and the instances of angelic intercourse with men are relied upon by millennarians to prove the possibility of effective intercourse or interposition by the risen saints in—yea, the most absolute control over the affairs of this world, without supposing them confined to it. They deny that it lies on them to show how such intercouse can or will take place, because the spiritualist is equally unable to explain these recorded facts which involve the same difficulty." —*Spirit of the Nineteenth Century, Extra.*

There is nothing then more irrational or mysterious, in the reign of the saints on earth or over earth, than there is in the appearances and rule of angels as recorded in scripture, or in the appearance of those who come out of their graves after our Lord's resurrection and appeared unto many in Jerusalem; or in the repeated apparitions of the Saviour in his raised body before his ascension, and to Paul and John afterward.

Nor is there, as shown above, any thing in millennarian views, to prevent the saints, if so ordered or permitted by their Lord, to visit on angel wings distant worlds and systems, to perform some message of mercy there, or to behold, as spectators, the glories of Godhead there revealed.

All this may be true, and vastly more, and yet in no way conflict with that government of the saints over a redeemed world in the new dispensation, which millennarians, in the light of scripture, contemplate.

Why should it then be thought a thing incredible, therefore, that when the once Crucified, shall come to add this revolted world, blood-bought, and cleansed, to his already immeasurably vast dominions, and to restore it to its proper place in the moral government of God, he should bring his redeemed people with him, raise their dead bodies, and transfigure them into his own glorious form, and then associate them with him in perfecting his great schemes of love to our world? Does he not now thus subordinately employ his people on earth, workers together with himself in saving men? And may he not exalt them to higher and more delightful powers in this same work in his kingdom, where no exhaustion or fatigue shall ever be experienced?

The scriptures, viewed in this light, teach that the glorified, are not to be mere idle spectators of Jehovah's glory, or the mere passive recipients of bliss poured into them, forcing out new songs of praise; but active agents in doing their Lord's will---ministering spirits in conveying the mandates of his love, or executing his pleasure in the government of the world. And there is accordingly a most wise adaptation in labors of love, and benevolent effort here in life, to prepare us for the kingdom of God, and to fit us for those higher services which we are to render in the future.

One more objection, often urged, must be noticed before we leave this chapter.

Millennarians generally maintain that the kingdom of God, or the kingdom of heaven, so much spoken of in scripture, is yet future, and is to be set up in full at the appearing of Jesus Christ. This is thought by some to be directly contrary to scripture, as the kingdom of God is very often spoken of as a present reality, and as therefore having been set up at the introduction of the gospel dispensation.

But it is also as often referred to as a future and glorious reality, in which the sanctified are to have their reward. To reconcile these, the kingdom of God is made to mean one thing in once place, and in the next passage another thing, and in a third something entirely different.

Now all these divers representations of scripture are entirely harmonious with millennarian views. The kingdom is a future reality, and yet a present one in purpose. Take an illustration. Suppose here was to be erected a great and splendid monument to Washington, from the voluntary offerings of all who wished to contribute; and to hasten the matter, suppose agents should be sent out into all parts of the country to solicit donations. Wherever they went, they would speak of the monument—the monument—and urge people to contribute to the monument, and thus their whole language would be as though there was in reality a monument already—and then again they would speak of the monument to be erected. Thus they would represent it as a present thing and still future, both of which would be true, rightly understood—existing in the present in plan or purpose, and to exist in the future as a splendid reality.

Or take another. Suppose here was a vacant territory, in which it was proposed to establish a new kingdom, composed of volunteers from all others. The king is appointed, the constitution published, and the fundamental laws enacted. By consent, ministers are sent out into all the world to persuade persons of a proper character to become members of this kingdom. As they went forth, they would urge persons to come into the kingdom. They would praise the king —explain the constitution and laws, set forth the great advantages and blessings to be derived by its subjects, and thus labor to induce men to enter. And thus they would necessarily speak of the kingdom as having a present existence, while in fact it only existed in purpose, and was to be set up at a future time, when the subjects to compose it had been gathered.

Just so the kingdom which the God of heaven will set up, exists now only in plan and purpose; but yet the Lord and his ministers, urge men to enter it as a present reality, and at the same time speak of it as future. Every true believer is a member of the kingdom, and Christ's ministers are now, and have been throughout the world, urging men to come in; and thus that great multitude is being gathered, to whom the government of the kingdom under Christ is to be given.

Now, let any one read the New Testament with this distinction clearly in his mind, and his eye on this future kingdom which the God of heaven will set up, and He will see how all the various representations of the kingdom harmoniously blend, without violence, in this one great and grand idea.

The existence of Christ's spiritual kingdom is not denied. It has existed in our world from Abel, the first who died in the faith, down through all succeeding time, and will continue to exist forever in all the sanctified, and his personal presence and visibly manifested glory, as in heaven, will only be the means of giving it a complete and perfect sway. "Beloved, now are we the sons of God, and it doth not yet appear what we shall be, but we know that when He doth appear, we shall be like him, for we shall see him as he is. And we know furthermore, for it is revealed, that we shall be kings and priests unto God, and shall reign upon the earth."—Rev. 5: 10.

It may be proper before closing, to notice one more objection which has been raised against the doctrine of the two resurrections advocated in this discourse. It is said, that the view which places the resurrection of the righteous before the thousand years, and of the unholy after this period, makes no provision for the resurrection of those who are righteous who die during the millennium. But we answer, it will be in time to answer this objection when it is proved that any of the righteous will die during this period. For myself, I have never seen any scripture which teaches that death will prevail among the sanctified, after the coming of our Lord, or during the millennium. The passage in Isaiah 65, does not prove it. It speaks of the child dying a hundred years old, and the *sinner* a hundred years old dying accursed; but it is not said that any of these are righteous. And hence the objection is founded only on an unauthorized assumption, and has no weight.

Chapter Sixth.

THE JEWS—THEIR CONVERSION AND RESTORATION, AND THE CONVERSION OF THE APPROVED GENTILE NATIONS AT THE COMING OF CHRIST.

To the Jews, under God, the Christian world is indebted for all the religious blessings and the immortal hopes they enjoy. Every sacred writer was a Jew. Patriarchs, and prophets, and apostles, whose bright example we have for imitation, and whose transcendent writings communicate to us the knowledge of God and the will of heaven, were all the seed of Abraham; and of them too, according to the flesh, Christ came, who is over all, God blessed forever.

When all God's purposes of mercy towards our dying world are accomplished, how truly and literally will the promise to the father of the faithful have been fulfilled, "In thee and in thy seed shall all the families of the earth be blessed." Can any fail to be interested in them, and in all God's revealed purposes respecting them?

That great and wonderful results are to be accomplished by them, and through them, in future ages, is clearly revealed, and for these God's providence has been over them, and has preserved them from destruction amid wars and revolutions, which have swept kingdoms and nations great and mighty, and their proud oppressors into oblivion. No powers leagued against them have been able to crush them —no fires of persecution kindled upon them, have availed to change or consume them; and no devices have succeeded in inducing them to abandon their peculiarities as a people, and become amalgamated with the nations among whom they have been dispersed. Their preservation in their wide dispersion, through so many centuries and perils, is a miracle of Providence, and clearly indicates some undeveloped destiny for which they are intended in unborn ages.

However any may attempt to account for their preservation as a distinct and peculiar people, the true solution of it is only to be found in the written word. In Jeremiah 31: 35–37, is the following declaration: "Thus saith the Lord, which giveth the sun for a light by day, and the ordinances of the moon and of the stars for a light by night, which divideth the sea when the waves thereof roar; the Lord of hosts is his name: if those ordinances depart from before me, saith the Lord, then the seed of Israel also shall cease from being a nation before me forever.

"Thus saith the Lord, if heaven above can be measured, and the foundations of the earth searched out beneath, I will also cast off the seed of Israel for all that they have done, saith the Lord."

And again the Lord says, 46: 27, 28, "But fear not thou, O my servant Jacob, and be not dismayed, O Israel: for behold I will save thee from afar off, and thy seed from the land of their captivity; and Jacob shall return and be in rest and at ease, and none shall make him afraid. Fear thou not, O Jacob my servant, saith the Lord: for I am with thee; for I will make a full end of all the nations whither I have driven thee: but I will not make a full end of thee, but correct thee in measure; yet will I not leave thee wholly unpunished."

In these and similar passages, the reason is clearly assigned why no powers, combined against the Jews for their destruction, have prospered, and why, while a full end has been made of mighty nations among which they have been scattered, they have been preserved.

How strong the language employed, and definite. Let

the nations put forth their power and skill against the ordinances of heaven. Let them, if they can, blot out the sun, or roll it backward in its course. Let them pluck the moon and the stars from their spheres, so that there shall be no more day and night, no more seed-time and harvest. When they can do these things, and not till then, will they be able to destroy the seed of Abraham and Jacob as a people.

And how strong the assurance here given that while these ordinances of heaven remain, and the sun, and the moon, and the stars remain in their spheres, and shed their effulgent glory on earth, the seed of Israel shall remain and multiply. While a full end will be made of all the nations among whom they are scattered and oppressed, they will stand the witnesses of a faithful, unchanging God.

The continued separate existence of the Jewish people, and the revealed purpose of God, that they shall remain so as firmly and certainly as the material universe, suggest the inference that the Lord must have some great and glorious end to be accomplished by and through them in the future. But independently of the prophecies, or some divine revelation, we could never know beforehand what this end or purpose was. Here, however, it is all clearly revealed. The good things which God has in store for them are as fully reveal as are the curses denounced, which have come upon them.

In addition to the plain and obvious import of the language in which their future glorious destiny is written, we have the assurance in the literality and faithfulness in which all the curses denounced have come upon them, that all the promises will be, in their time and order, as literally and faithfully accomplished.

No one doubts the literal truth of the curses denounced against them in the 28th chapter of Deuteronomy, and in the prophets generally. "Now the Jew has found it to be no overdrawn or chimerical picture, but a most certain and appalling reality that judgment was written against him in the oracles of God. We conclude, therefore, by whatever truth and consistency there is in these oracles of God, that the same Jew must be destined to know it as an equally certain and faithful reality, that he is written there also the subject of distinguished favor, blessing, and glory."

"If, in reading the prophecies which have been put on record concerning God's ancient people, I find it predicted in terms the most express, that they were to be cut off from the church, torn from their native land, dispersed among all the nations, a reproach, a proverb, and a by-word, and still be preserved amid all their calamities, a distinct and peculiar people; and if, in searching into history, I also find that the whole, to the very letter, has been verified—shall I doubt, when on reading further in the same line of prophecy, I find it written in terms equally express, that they are to be reunited to the church of God, reinstated in their ancient heritage, and there be invested with an honor and a glory, which had no parallel in their days of by-gone magnificence?

"When I see that God has magnified his faithfulness in giving to the dark side of their history the most literal and complete verification, can I think so meanly of the consistency of his prophetic word, as to suppose that he will not also verify, to the letter, the other and brighter side, but allow it to pass away into some vague generality?"

But the principle here advocated, is established by the authority of God himself. By the prophet Jeremiah, 32 : 42, it is thus written, "For thus saith the Lord: Like as I have brought this great evil upon this people, so will I bring upon them all the good that I have promised them."

Jehovah here declares that he will fulfill all the promises of good that he has made to them, in the same manner that he has accomplished upon them all the evil he threatened.

In the light, then, of God's own exposition, we have only to read the prophetic promises he has made, to know of a certainty for what the Jews are preserved, and what is to be their future and glorious destiny.

We see that God has fulfilled his word thus far in their remarkable preservation, and we may hence argue the remainder in its time.

1. It is predicted that the children of Israel as a nation and people, shall all yet be converted to Christ, that they shall yet be reingrafted into their own olive tree, from which they were broken for unbelief after their rejection of the Messiah.

The limits assigned to this discussion, will only admit a part of the testimony on this subject.

Jeremiah, 31: 31–34. "Behold, the days come, saith the Lord, that I will make a new covenant with the house of Israel, and with the house of Judah: Not according to the covenant that I made with their fathers, in the day that I took them by the hand to bring them out of the land of Egypt; which my covenant they broke, although I was a husband unto them, saith the Lord: But this shall be the covenant that I will make with the house of Israel: After those days, saith the Lord, I will put my law in their inward parts, and write it in their hearts; and will be their God, and they shall be my people. And they shall teach no more every man his neighbor, and every man his brother, saying, know the Lord: for they shall all know me, from the least of them unto the greatest of them, saith the Lord: for I will forgive them their iniquity, and I will remember their sin no more."

That this is a prediction of the future conversion of the Jews as a people, is manifest from the whole discourse of the prophet in connection with which it stands. The whole house of Israel, the people, whom the Lord once took by the hand, and led forth out of the land of Egypt, are the subjects, and the only subjects, of the prediction; for they only are named: and it manifestly has never yet been fulfilled.

No era in their history, either before or after the Babylonish captivity answers in any degree to that state of exalted and universal piety here revealed. At this period, God's law is to be put in their inward parts and written in their hearts, and all are to know and serve the Lord, from the least unto the greatest. No language could more definitely and certainly foretel their individual and universal conversion. And as surely as the Lord has brought upon them all the great evils they have suffered, in accordance with his denunciations, so certainly will he yet accomplish for them all that he has promised.

Hosea, 3: 4, 5. "For the children of Israel shall abide many days without a king, and without a prince, and without a sacrifice, and without an image, and without an ephod, and without a teraphim: Afterward shall the children of Israel return, and seek the Lord their God, and David their king; and shall fear the Lord and his goodness, in the latter days."

This is a remarkable prediction, and has, in part, been as remarkably fulfilled. The prophecy declares that for many days, or for a long time prior to their conversion, they should remain without an altar or sacrifice, without a priesthood, without any divine oracle, or any of the divinely constituted ordinances of religion.

Now, how literally and affectingly has all this been fulfilled, since their last wide and melancholy dispersion.

When Christ suffered on the cross, their priesthood, and their ordinances of divine appointment for the purposes then constituted, were set aside by their fulfillment in him; and by their persevering rejection of the Messiah, and the gospel, they were left without any divinely appointed ordinances of religion.

And this has remained for many days. Through 1800

years of dispersion and sorrow, they have remained without a priesthood, a sacrifice, or any means of grace appointed in the gospel.

But this will not always be true of them. He who so exactly foretold their state during their dispersion, has said, "that the children of Israel shall return and seek the Lord their God, and David their king, and shall fear the Lord and his goodness in the latter days." How clearly and strikingly is their conversion to Christ here foretold, under the name and title of David their king. There cannot be a reasonable doubt but that Christ, the King of Israel, to whom the Lord God is to give the throne of his father David, is here meant.

"It was the usage of the Hebrews to transfer the name of an ancestor to his posterity. Thus Jacob and Israel are used as the names of the whole descendants collectively; and Joseph, Judah, Benjamin, Ephraim, and others, as the names of their several tribes. In accordance with this custom, the name David, the *parent of the monarchy of Israel*, of which Christ was to spring, is, in the judgment of commentators generally, used as his denominative, as the prince of his family, whom God was to raise up to sit on his throne forever. And it was peculiarly proper, inasmuch as he was the only descendant of David who was to hold the sceptre of that people, after the period of this prophecy; Zedekiah, the last of that line, having already been deposed and carried into captivity, and his sons, who might have inherited his throne, had the nation regained its independence, exterminated."—LORD.

In the latter days, then, when they are brought to fear the Lord and his goodness, they are, in a peculiar sense, to seek for David or Christ their king, who shall be their deliverer and salvation.

The prophet Ezekiel foretels, with great explicitness, their conversion and entire and universal sanctification, 36: 21–31.

"But I had pity for my holy name, which the house of Israel had profaned among the heathen, whither they went. Therefore say unto the house of Israel, thus saith the Lord God; I do not this for your sakes, O house of Israel, but for my holy name's sake, which ye have profaned among the heathen, whither ye went. And I will sanctify my great name, which was profaned among the heathen, which ye have profaned in the midst of them; and the heathen shall know that I am the Lord, saith the Lord God, when I shall be sanctified in you before their eyes.

"For I will take you from among the heathen, and gather you out of all countries, and will bring you into your own land. Then will I sprinkle clean water upon you, and ye shall be clean: from all your filthiness, and from all your idols, will I clean you. A new heart also will I give you, and a new spirit will I put within you: and I will take away the stony heart out of your flesh, and will give you a heart of flesh. And I will put my spirit within you, and cause you to walk in my statutes, and ye shall keep my judgments, and do them. And ye shall dwell in the land that I gave to your fathers; and ye shall be my people, and I will be your God. I will also save you from all your uncleanness: and I will call for the corn, and increase it, and lay no famine upon you. And I will multiply the fruit of the tree, and the increase of the field, that ye shall receive no more reproach of famine among the heathen. Then shall ye remember your own evil ways, and your doings that were not good, and shall loathe yourselves in your own sight for your iniquities, and for your abominations. Thus saith the Lord God: In the day that I shall have cleansed you from all your iniquities, I will also cause you to dwell in the cities, and the wastes shall be builded. And the desolate land shall be tilled, whereas it lay desolate in the sight of all that passed by."

The prophetic promises, contained in this most interesting

passage, are often applied to the Gentiles indiscriminately with the Jews ; but for this there is certainly no warrant.

The Gentiles are not named in the prophecy, except as those among whom the Israelites are scattered, and out from among whom they are to be gathered, to be restored to Palestine.

The children of Israel are distinctly named—and they to whom the promises are directed, are the people, who, for their sins, were dispersed among the heathen. The restoration and universal sanctification here described, are manifestly yet future, for they have never yet been fulfilled in the manner and to the extent predicted. The return of the Jews from their Babylonish captivity did not realize these promises, for they were not then cleansed from all their iniquities, and made holy, prosperous and happy, in their own land.

The discussion of this subject by the apostle Paul, and his quotations from these prophetic promises to prove his position, show that the predicted universal conversion and sanctification of Israel is yet future.

Romans 11 : 25-28. " For I would not, Brethren, that ye should be ignorant of this mystery, lest ye should be wise in your own conceits, that blindness in part is happened to Israel, until the fullness of the Gentiles be come in. And so all Israel shall be saved : as it is written, There shall come out of Zion the deliverer, and shall turn away ungodliness from Jacob : For this is my covenant unto them, when I shall take away their sins. As concerning the gospel, they are enemies for your sakes : but as touching the election, they are beloved for the father's sake."

Let the reader notice, that it is the house of Jacob, the children of Israel, who have been broken off from their own olive tree, that the Gentiles might be grafted in, who are the subjects of these prophetic promises. It is not God's spiritual Israel, therefore, that is here meant, whose conversion and salvation are foretold, but the literal Jew, to whom blindness in part hath happened for a time, until the fullness of the Gentiles be come in. The Jews and Gentiles are carefully kept distinct in all these prophecies, and the portion designed for each is given in order and due season. But—

2. Not only is their conversion foretold as a people, and their universal sanctification, but the means especially by which the great work is to effected. Ezekiel clearly intimates these in a prediction already quoted, where it is declared, that God, in a special manner, will interpose for their salvation by the agency of his Truth and Spirit.

The prophet Zechariah, 12: 9–14, and 13: 1, records a remarkable promise of God to Israel, in the day when Jerusalem shall be made a cup of trembling unto all the people round about, and when all who come against her, and burden themselves with her, shall be destroyed.

"In that day shall the Lord defend the inhabitants of Jerusalem; and he that is feeble among them at that day, shall be as David; and the house of David shall be as God, as the angel of the Lord before them.

"And it shall come to pass in that day, that I will seek to destroy all the nations that come against Jerusalem. And I will pour upon the house of David, and upon the inhabitants of Jerusalem, the spirit of grace and of supplications; and they shall look upon me whom they have pierced, and they shall mourn for Him, as one mourneth for his only son, and shall be in bitterness for him, as one that is in bitterness for his first-born.

"In that day shall there be a great mourning in Jerusalem, as the mourning of Hadadrimmon, in the valley of Megiddon. And the land shall mourn, every family apart; the family of the house of David apart, and their wives apart; the family of the house of Nathan apart, and their wives apart; the family of the house of Levi apart, and their wives apart; the family of Shemei apart, and their wives apart; all the families that remain, every family apart, and their wives apart.

"In that day, there shall be a fountain opened to the house of David, and to the inhabitants of Jerusalem, for sin and for uncleanness."

What a wonderful revival of religion is here predicted, when all the families of Israel, by the appearing of Him whom they have pierced, and by the outpourings of God's Spirit, shall be convinced of their unbelief and sin, and shall seek, in secret places, to pour out their agonized hearts in prayer to God for pardon and salvation. And when the fountain of God's revealed and promised love and mercy is opened for them in that day, what acclamations of joy will be heard ascending from thousands of renewed souls, and how, through them will glory redound to God and flow through the nations! In this prediction, we have all the characteristics of a genuine and powerful revival of religion, in which the power of God and the renewing influences of his Spirit, shall be put forth for the conversion of all Israel.

Many other predictions, having a special reference to the conversion and sanctification of the whole Jewish people at some future period, and for which they are preserved, might be quoted, but these are sufficient to prove the point. No language could foretel such a result, more clearly, than it is affirmed by Him who cannot lie in these various scriptures. Every one of them, from the least of them unto the greatest of them, is yet to know the Lord Jesus, and so universal will this be, that no one shall have cause or occasion to say to his brother or neighbor, know the Lord. But:—

3. Their restoration to their own land and their reëstablishment there, in peace, purity and prosperity forever, is in

the promise, made consequent on their conversion, and uniformly and inseparably connected with it.

In the twenty-eighth chapter of Deuteronomy, there are many curses denounced against the Jews, should they ever refuse obedience to God, and do the things forbidden. History informs us they did transgress, and the threatened curses have come upon them literally, and to the utmost. But in chapter 30: 1, 7, Moses says, "And it shall come to pass, when all these things are come upon thee, the blessing and the curse, which I have set before thee, and thou shalt call them to mind among all the nations whither the Lord thy God hath driven thee; and shalt return unto the Lord thy God, and shalt obey his voice according to all that I command thee this day, thou and thy children, with all thy heart, and with all thy soul; that then, the Lord thy God will turn thy captivity, and have compassion upon thee, and will return and gather thee from all the nations whither the Lord thy God hath scattered thee.

"If any of thine be driven out unto the utmost parts of heaven, from thence will the Lord thy God gather thee, and from thence will he fetch thee.

"And the Lord thy God will bring thee into the land which thy fathers possessed, and thou shalt possess it: and he will do thee good, and multiply thee above thy fathers.

"And the Lord thy God will circumcise thy heart, and the heart of thy seed, to love the Lord thy God with all thy heart, and with all thy soul, that thou mayest live.

"And the Lord thy God will put all these curses upon thine enemies, and on them that hate thee, which persecuted thee. And thou shalt return and obey the voice of the Lord, and do all his commandments which I command thee this day."

Here, then, is a most solemn pledge on the part of God,

that whenever, among all the nations whither they are driven for their sins, they shall repent and return unto the Lord, the Lord will restore them from their captivity, and bring them again into the land which their fathers possessed, even though they be driven out unto the uttermost parts of heaven.

But, it has been shown, that they are all yet to be brought to repentance, and to be universally and individually sanctified; therefore, when their conversion takes place, God will be bound by his own solemn promise, recorded as a standing testimony by Moses, to restore them, and to give them there, in their own land, all the prosperity predicted. If he does not, his word will fail; but this cannot be; for heaven and earth shall sooner pass away, than one jot or tittle fail from the law till all be fulfilled.

In accordance with the promise given by God through Moses, we find that their complete and full restoration to their land as an eternal possession, is almost uniformly foretold in connection with their sanctification. Their predicted restoration is so explicit and circumstantial that it would seem a proposition could not be framed to declare it more certainly.

Jeremiah 23: 1–8. "Wo be unto the pastors that destroy and scatter the sheep of my pasture! saith the Lord. Therefore thus saith the Lord God of Israel against the pastors that feed my people; ye have scattered my flock, and driven them away, and have not visited them: behold I will visit upon you the evil of your doings, saith the Lord. And I will gather the remnant of my flock out of all countries whither I have driven them, and will bring them again to their folds; and they shall be fruitful and increase.

"And I will set up shepherds over them, which shall feed them: and they shall fear no more, nor be dismayed, neither shall they be lacking, saith the Lord.

"Behold, the days come, saith the Lord, that I will raise unto David a righteous branch, and a king shall reign and prosper, and shall execute judgment and justice in the earth. In his days Judah shall be saved, and Israel shall dwell safely: and this is the name whereby he shall be called, The Lord our Righteousness. Therefore, behold, the days come, saith the Lord, that they shall no more say, The Lord liveth which brought up and which led the seed of the house of Israel out of the north country, and from all the countries whither I had driven them; and they shall dwell in their own land."

Commentators are uniformly agreed that the Lord Jesus Christ is intended by The Lord our Righteousness in this passage; and this fact clearly shows that the restoration predicted is still future; for "it was to take place after the Messiah was raised up as a branch unto David, and therefore after his birth. But no such restoration has been accomplished since Christ's first advent. So far from it, the final dispersion of the Jews did not take place till after his ascension, and they and the other tribes still continue in exile from their native land." And the futurity of its fulfillment is still further manifest from the fact that it is not to take place till Christ's second advent, as his reign, under which it is to be accomplished, is to be on the earth. It is on the earth that he is to reign and prosper, and execute judgment and justice as the branch unto David; for it is on the throne of David that he is to exercise his administration over Israel, as is manifest from a parallel passage found in chap. 33: 15–17.

"Behold, the days come, saith the Lord, that I will perform that good thing which I have promised unto the house of Israel, and to the house of Judah. In those days, and at that time, will I cause the Branch of Righteousness to grow up unto David; and he shall execute judgment and righteousness *in the land. In those days* shall Judah be saved, and Jerusalem shall dwell safely; and this is the name wherewith he shall be called, The Lord our Righteousness. For thus saith the Lord, David shall never want a man to sit upon the throne of the house of Israel."

"It is in the days of his reign on the throne of David, therefore, in Judea, that this prophecy is to receive its accomplishment, and thence after his second coming." As was shown in a previous chapter, "It cannot be said that Christ now sits on the throne of David. Instead, he sits with the Father on his throne. David's throne was the throne of the Israelitish nations in Palestine, not the throne of the universe. To ascribe to him that throne, were to deify him by ascribing to him the prerogatives and government of the Almighty."

This is clearly, then, a prediction of the return and reorganization of the Israelites as a nation, subsequent to Christ's second advent, and commencement of his millennial reign on earth.

There are many passages which show a yet future restoration of the seed of Abraham. On this point a few more quotations only will be made.

Thus, in Jeremiah, chap. 30: 1–10, a restoration is predicted, which is never to be followed by any further subjugation to enemies or strangers.

"Thus saith the Lord God of Israel, saying, Write thou all the words that I have spoken unto thee in a book. For lo, the days come, saith the Lord, that I will bring again the captivity of my people Israel and Judah, saith the Lord. And I will cause them to return to the land that I gave to their fathers, and they shall possess it. For it shall come to pass in that day, saith the Lord of hosts, I will break his yoke from off thy neck, and will burst thy bonds, and strangers shall no more serve themselves of him. But they shall serve the Lord their God, and David their king, whom I will raise up unto them. Therefore, fear thou not, O my servant Jacob, saith the Lord, neither be dismayed, O Israel, for lo, I will save thee from afar, and thy seed from the land of thy captivity; and Jacob shall return, and shall be in rest and be quiet, and none shall make him afraid. For I am with thee, saith the Lord, to save thee: though I make a full end of all the nations whither I have scattered thee, yet will I not make a full end of thee; but I will correct thee in measure, and will not leave thee altogether unpunished."

A comparison of this prediction with the miserable condition, and long and almost perpetual vassalage of the Jewish nation after their return in part from Babylon, will show that this prediction did not meet its fulfillment at that period; and as there has been no return of captivity since, it must yet be future.

And let it be remembered that God has said, "Like as I have brought all this great evil upon this people, so will I bring upon them all the good that I have promised them."

But should any doubt or deny the possibility of their restoration, or stumble at the difficulties which lie in the way, on account of their wide dispersion and the apparent loss of the ten tribes; even this despondency and unbelief were foreseen, and its possibility and certainty demonstrated by the Lord himself, that Jew nor Gentile might question the ability of the Almighty to fulfill his word.

The vision of the resurrection of the dry bones, Ezekiel 37: 1–14, was designed to show to the Jews in their dispersion, and to all others, that the power of God is abundantly able to accomplish all that he has promised respecting their salvation and restoration.

"The hand of the Lord was upon me, and carried me out in the spirit of the Lord, and set me down in the midst of the valley which was full of bones, and caused me to pass by them round about: and behold, there were very many in the open valley; and lo, they were very dry. And he said unto me, Son of man, can these bone live? and I answered, O Lord God, thou knowest. Again he said unto me, Prophecy upon these bones, and say unto them, O ye dry bones, hear the word of the Lord. Thus saith the Lord God unto these bones: Behold, I will cause breath to enter into you, and ye shall live: And I will lay sinews upon you, and will bring up flesh upon you, and cover you with skin, and put breath in you, and ye shall live; and ye shall know that I am the Lord. So I prophesied as I was commanded: and as I prophesied, there was a noise, and behold a shaking, and the bones came together, bone to his bone.

"And when I beheld, lo, the sinews and the flesh came up upon them, and the skin covered them above: but there was no breath in them.

"Then said he unto me, Prophecy unto the wind, prophecy, son of man, and say to the wind, Thus saith the Lord God: Come from the four winds, O breath, and breathe upon these slain, that they may live. So I prophesied as he commanded me, and the breath came into them, and they lived, and stood up upon their feet, an exceeding great army."

But what does this vision illustrate, and to what was it designed to apply? Not to the conversion of sinners, or the revival of dead and dried up churches; but to the conversion and restoration of Israel. For thus it is immediately added in explanation, and application.

"Then said he unto me, Son of man, these bones are," or represent, "the whole house of Israel: behold, they say, our bones are dried, and our hope is lost: we are cut off for our parts. Therefore, prophecy and say unto them, Thus saith the Lord God; Behold, O my people, I will open your graves, and cause you to come up out of your graves, and *bring you into the land of Israel.* And ye shall know that I am the Lord, when I have opened your graves, O my people, and brought you up out of your graves, and shall put my spirit in you, and ye shall live, and I shall place you in your own land: then shall ye know that I, the Lord, have spoken it, and performed it, saith the Lord."

Here, then, the design and application of the vision is rendered definite and certain. And that its design was to show the certainty and possibility of the conversion, and especially the restoration of the whole Jewish nation to their own land, is rendered also certain, from the fact that these are the great themes of prophecy in the verses and chapters immediately preceding the vision.

It matters not, then, how many obstacles and difficulties, in human estimation, are in the way of the literal and faithful accomplishment of these promises. God, who can raise the dead to life, can bring them up, wherever dispersed, and cause them to dwell in their own land. And when all these things are fulfilled, what a sublime demonstration it will be, before the world and the universe, of the truth and faithfulness of God: and how truly will all then know that the God of Israel is the Lord, worthy to be trusted, and had in reverence by all that are round about him!

But not only are the fact and certainty of their restoration foretold, but the means and agencies, in many particulars, by which it is to be effected.

Isaiah 11: 10–16. "And in that day there shall be a root of Jesse, which shall stand for an ensign to the people; to it shall the Gentiles seek: and his rest shall be glorious. And it shall come to pass in that day, that the Lord shall set his hand again the second time to recover the remnant of his people, which shall be left, from Assyria, and from Egypt, and from Pathros, and from Cush, and from Elam, and Shinar, and from Hamath, and from the islands of the sea.

"And he shall set up an ensign for the nations, and shall

assemble the outcasts of Israel, and gather together the dispersed of Judah from the *four corners of the earth.* The envy also of Ephraim shall depart, and the adversaries of Judah shall be cut off: Ephraim shall not vex Judah, and Judah shall not vex Ephraim. But they shall fly upon the shoulders of the Philistines toward the west; and they shall spoil them of the east together: they shall lay their hands upon Edom and Moab; and the children of Ammon shall obey them. And the Lord shall utterly destroy the tongue of the Egyptian sea, and with his mighty wind shall he shake his hand over the river, and shall smite in the seven streams, and make men go over dry shod. And there shall be an highway for the remnant of his people, which shall be left from Assyria; like as it was to Israel in the day that he came up out of the land of Egypt."

"And in that day thou shalt say, O Lord, I will praise thee: though thou wast angry with me, thine anger is turned away, and thou comfortest me. Behold, God is my salvation: I will trust, and not be afraid: for the Lord Jehovah is my strength and my song; he also is become my salvation. Therefore with joy shall ye draw water out of the wells of salvation." 12: 1-6.

Now there is no possibility of consistently accommodating this prediction to the return of the Jews from Babylon, or to their simple introduction to the Christian church, or any past event in their history. For—

1. It is a second restoration that is spoken of, whereas that from Babylon was the first.

2. It is a restoration that is to take place at the time that a rod comes forth from the stem of Jesse, upon whom the Spirit of the Lord is to rest, and who is to judge or rule the poor with righteousness, and reprove with equity for the meek of the earth; and also at the time that the wolf is to dwell with the lamb, and the leopard lie down with the kid, and the

earth be filled with the knowledge of the Lord as the waters cover the sea, and when there shall be nothing to hurt or destroy in all God's holy mountain.

And all this shows that it is a yet future event, and is to be brought about in a peculiar manner by the coming of Christ, the Rod of Jesse—which shall stand for an ensign to the people.

3. It is a restoration, which is to be effected with some such miraculous displays, as was the deliverance of Israel from Egyptian bondage; as is manifest from verse fifteen: "And the Lord shall utterly destroy the tongue of the Egyptian sea, and with his mighty wind shall he shake his hand over the river, and shall smite it in the seven streams, and make men go over dry shod. And there shall be an highway for the remnant of his people, which shall be left from Assyria;" like as it was to Israel in the day that he came up out of the land of Egypt.

4. In accomplishing God's purpose in this restoration, the children of Ammon and surrounding nations, are to be brought to coöperate.

All these considerations show that it is a yet future glorious reality that is pointed to.

The prophecies are very express in declaring that the Gentile nations shall all be workers together with God, in accomplishing the restoration of Israel—and if any will not, they shall perish.

Isah, 49: 22, 23. "Thus saith the Lord God, Behold, I will lift up mine hand to the Gentiles, and set my standard to the people: and they shall bring thy sons in their arms, and thy daughters shall be carried upon their shoulders. And kings shall be thy nursing fathers, and queens thy nursing mothers: they shall bow down to thee with their face toward the earth, and lick up the dust of thy feet; and thou shalt know that I am the Lord: for they shall not be ashamed that wait for me."

This language is, no doubt, somewhat figurative, drawn from the manner in which subjection was sometimes manifested, in the times in which the prophet wrote; but the great idea intended to be conveyed, is obvious, which is, that these Gentiles, with their kings and queens, will be made instrumental in protecting, supporting, and restoring his scattered and downtrodden people to their own land. Nor does the language imply, that the service which they will be called upon to render, will be unwilling, degrading, or burdensome. On the contrary, it will manifestly be in great love and kindness.

"And they shall bring thy sons in their arms, and thy daughters or little ones shall be carried upon their shoulders." Could kind attention and caressing tenderness be more touchingly expressed!

The ships of commercial nations are also to be employed, and all the various means of conveyance in use, in different countries. In the sixtieth chapter of Isaiah, all this is beautifully and graphically foretold, in connection with their entire sanctification, and the conversion of the Gentile nations who shall at that time submit to Jesus, and yield themselves obediently to the Lord.

Verses 8–22. The prophet seems to be represented as standing on some eminence, overlooking the broad expanse of the Mediterranean; and seeing it whitened with the spreading canvas of numerous fleets, borne rapidly before the breeze towards the shores of Palestine, he exclaims:

"Who are these that fly as a cloud, and as the doves to their windows? Surely the Isles shall wait for me, and the ships of Tarshish first, to bring thy sons from far, their silver and their gold with them, unto the name of the Lord thy God, and the Holy One of Israel, because he hath glorified thee. And the sons of strangers shall build up thy walls, and their kings shall minister unto thee; for in my wrath I smote thee, but in my favor have I had mercy upon thee.

"Therefore shall thy gates be open continually; they shall not be shut day nor night; that men may bring unto thee the forces of the Gentiles, and that their kings may be brought. For the nation and kingdom that will not serve thee shall perish; yea, those nations shall be utterly wasted. The glory of Lebanon shall come unto thee, the fir-tree, the pine-tree, and the box together, to beautify the place of my sanctuary; and I will make the place of my feet glorious.

"The sons also of them that afflicted thee shall come bending unto thee: and all they that despised thee shall bow themselves down at the soles of thy feet; and they shall call thee, The city of the Lord, The Zion of the Holy One of Israel. Whereas thou hast been forsaken and hated, so that no man went through thee, I will make thee an eternal excellency, a joy of many generations.

"For I know their works and their thoughts; it shall come, that I will gather all nations and tongues; and they shall come and see my glory.

"And I will set a sign among them, and will send those that escape of them unto the nations, to Tarshish, to Pul, and Lud, that draw the bow, to Tubal, and Javon, to the isles afar off, that have not heard my fame, neither have seen my glory; and they shall declare my glory among the Gentiles.

"And they shall bring all your brethren for an offering unto the Lord, out of all nations, upon horses, and in chariots, and in litters, and upon mules, and upon swift beasts, to my holy mountain, Jerusalem, saith the Lord, as the children of Israel bring an offering in a clean vessel unto the house of the Lord."—Is., 66: 18–20.

What a sight will here be presented when the Lord shall erect on Mount Zion, the ensign, and shall shake his hand over the nations, and bid them bring his exiled people home and to Jerusalem, as an offering unto the Lord, for all the injuries they have done them. Then, indeed, will he say to the north, give up; and to the south, keep not back; bring my sons from afar, and my daughters from the ends of the earth.

Thus clearly is it predicted, that all Israel shall yet be converted, and restored to their own land, and there made an eternal excellency. And all this will be brought about by means fully adequate to the great and grand result. The Lord our Righteousness will himself appear for their deliverance and salvation, and will rule upon the throne of David, and as his kingdom is a kingdom of means, he will, by the mighty influences which he will bring to bear upon them, cause all the Gentile nations joyfully to aid by every mode of travel and conveyance, and by their combined wealth, in their restoration and reorganization as a great and glorious people, whose God, henceforth and forever, shall be the Lord Christ.

But a small portion of the evidence upon this subject has been presented. It is one of the great burdens of prophecy, around which cluster the hopes of a world lying in wickedness, and the salvation of unborn and countless millions.

That all this will take place, in connection with the glorious personal appearing of the Son of David, is manifest—

1. From the fact, that his coming is to be pre-millennial, as has been proved. The conversion and restoration of the Jews are uniformly associated in scripture with the entire conversion and restoration of the world.

Thus in Is. 60: 18–22, in connection with their restoration, it is said: "Violence shall no more be heard in thy land, wasting nor destruction within thy borders; but thou shalt call thy walls Salvation, and thy gates Praise. The sun shall be no more thy light by day: neither for brightness shall the moon give light unto thee: but the Lord shall be unto thee an everlasting light, and thy God thy glory. Thy sun shall no more go down; neither shall thy moon withdraw itself: for the Lord shall be thine *everlasting* light, and the days of thy mourning shall be ended. Thy people also shall be all righteous: *They shall inherit the land forever*, the branch of my planting, the work of my hands, that I may be glorified."

But the fulfillment of all this will be the millennium, and as Christ is to come before this, it is certain that this glorious and perfect restoration and sanctification of the Jewish people must be connected with the coming of the Lord.

2. It is evident that the restoration and rebuilding of Jerusalem must be after the advent, from the fact that they are to take place in the new heavens and the new earth.

Is. 66: 17–19. "For behold I create a new heavens and a new earth: and the former shall not be remembered, nor come into mind. But be ye glad and rejoice forever in that which I create: for behold, I create Jerusalem a rejoicing, and her people a joy. And I will rejoice in Jerusalem, and joy in my people: and the voice of weeping shall no more be heard in her, nor the voice of crying." But this new heavens and new earth, in which Jerusalem is to be made a rejoicing, &c., according to the express teaching of Peter, 2 Epis. 3: 13, is to take place after the coming of the Lord, and as the result of the conflagration there predicted; and therefore the restoration of the Jews as a people, and their sanctification, must be after his advent.

3. We are assured, in various scriptures already quoted, that their conversion and restoration are to be at the time that a righteous Branch—the Lord our Righteousness is raised up unto them: and also at the time that the Lord God will give unto him the throne of his Father David, and at the time that Christ, as king, is to reign and prosper, and execute justice and judgment in the land; and all these

jointly prove the pre-millennial advent, and that the glorious appearing of our Lord will mark the epoch of Israel's deliverance and eternal salvation.

4. In harmony with the inference drawn from the above scriptures, it is predicted that the appearance of the Lord will be a means, in connection with the outpourings of the Spirit, of their awakening, conviction and conversion.—Zech. 12: 10. "And they shall look upon me whom they have pierced, and mourn." Rev. 1: 9. "Behold he cometh with clouds, and every eye shall see him, and they also which pierced him."

The glorious appearing of our Lord will be just as wisely and benevolently adapted to their awakening and conversion, as was his appearance to the apostle Paul on his way to Damascus, and it is presumed will have just the same influence and no more.

It is not to undervalue the Spirit, to ascribe an efficient awakening and convincing agency to the coming of our Lord; for does not God often employ solemn providences to awaken sinners, now, and did he not employ miraculous demonstrations on the day of Pentecost? And when the Jews, in their wide dispersion, shall have all their unbelief and delusions scattered by the coming of the Son of Man, and then indeed look upon him whom they have pierced, and mourn—oh, what bitterness of soul will overwhelm them in deep confession and repentance! and how then will salvation flow to them as a river, and righteousness as the waves of the sea!

But when the Jews are converted and restored, it will not be for themselves alone, but only a fulfillment in an enlarged sense, of the ancient promise to Abraham: "And in thee, and in thy seed, shall all the nations of the earth be blessed." When the Lord comes, there will be apostate nations, and many perhaps among all, who will not receive the Saviour, and who will be cut off from the earth. These will be treated of in the next chapter. But all Gentile nations and remnants of nations, who receive the Messiah as their king and Saviour, will be made sharers in Jerusalem's blessedness and glory, and through all the long ages that shall follow, the seed of Abraham shall be made a joy and blessing to the world.

For proof, turn first to Isaiah 2 : 2–5. And now, in reading this passage, let the reader suppose that the Jews are restored, Jerusalem re-built, and the Lord's house exalted there upon the top of the highest mountain, in which the personal presence and glory of the Lord is manifested ; and then, with this great idea in his mind, see how natural, and simple, and beautiful is the description :

"And it shall come to pass in the last days, that the mountain of the Lord's house shall be established in the top of the mountains, that is on Mount Toriah, and shall be exalted above the hills; *and all nations* shall flow unto it. And many people shall go and say, Come ye, and *let us* go up to the mountain of the Lord, to the house of the God of Jacob ; and he will teach *us* his ways, and we will walk in his paths : for out of Sion shall go forth the law, and the word of the Lord from Jerusalem."

And what shall be the result of all this ? "And he shall judge among these nations, that come up, and shall rebuke many people :" and then, as the result, they shall go home, "and beat their swords into plough-shares, and their spears into pruning-hooks : nation shall not lift up sword against nation, neither shall they learn war any more."

Now, how clearly does this passage predict the participation of many Gentile people in Jerusalem's blessedness and glory, when a king there shall reign and prosper, and shall execute righteousness and justice in the earth ? And what a sight it will be for angels to look down upon, and for God to smile over, to see the nations exhorting one another, "come ye, and let us go up to the mountain of the Lord, to the house of the God of Jacob; and he will teach us his ways, and we will walk in his paths." And will it be unworthy of God, the Saviour, to give the world such a demonstration of love and truth, by his personal presence and glory, as shall lead them thus joyfully to come up to receive instruction from his lips, and to yield themselves obediently to his laws? Is not such a manifestation just what the world needs, and what we might, at some time, expect, from a Being of infinite compassion and love?

The participation of the Gentile world in the blessedness of Messiah's reign, when Jerusalem shall be restored, and the Lord our Righteousness seated upon the throne of David, is described in strong and glowing language, in Isaiah 54: 1–4:

"Sing, O barren, thou that didst not bear; break forth into singing, and cry aloud, thou that didst not travail with child: for more are the children of the desolate, than the children of the married wife, saith the Lord. Enlarge the place of thy tent, and let them stretch forth the curtains of thine habitation; spare not, lengthen thy cords, and strengthen thy stakes: For thou shalt break forth on the right hand, and on the left; and thy seed shall inherit the Gentiles, and make the desolate cities to be inhabited."

The blessings of Israel are here compared to a tent, which they are required to stretch forth and enlarge, until its amplitude shall be sufficient to accommodate the world. Thus will the arms of Jacob's mercy and Israel's Redeemer be yet stretched forth to embrace the wide world, when all nations shall flow into the church, of which the restored and sanctified Jews shall be the centre and an eternal excellency. And, oh, what acclamations of exulting joy will then go up from a renewed world, and be reëchoed through the universe!

Turn over now to Isaiah 60 : 1–7, and see how beautifully and exultingly the same thing is there predicted. "Arise, shine, for thy light is come, and the glory of the Lord is risen upon thee. For behold, the darkness shall cover the earth, and gross darkness the people; but the Lord shall arise upon thee, and his glory shall be upon thee. And the Gentiles shall come to thy light, and kings to the brightness of thy rising.

"Lift up thine eyes round about, and see: all they gather themselves together, they come to thee; thy sons shall come from far, and thy daughters shall be nursed at thy side. Then shalt thou see, and flow together, and thine heart shall fear and be enlarged; because the abundance of the sea shall be converted unto thee, the forces of the Gentiles shall come unto thee. The multitude of camels shall cover thee, the dromedaries of Midian and Ephah; all they from Sheba shall come; they shall bring gold and incense; and they shall show forth the praises of the Lord. And all the flocks of Kedar shall be gathered together unto thee, the rams of Nebaioth shall minister unto thee: they shall come up with acceptance on mine altar, and I will glorify the house of my glory."

And, thus it will come to pass, as predicted, Is. 66 : 23, that, in the new heavens and the new earth, which God will create, "That from one new moon to another, and from one Sabbath to another, shall all flesh come to worship before me, saith the Lord."

No language could more forcibly and clearly predict, that in Israel's future glory and exaltation, all the world shall participate, and that in the seed of Abraham, all the families of the earth shall be forever blessed.

Many more scriptures might be produced in proof; but these are deemed sufficient. Should any object, that these prophecies which have been quoted belong to the church, be it so, but they undoubtedly refer to a future condition and state of the church; and at the time to which they refer, all Israel shall be reingrafted into their own olive tree, and hence they will be the church, to which converted Gentile nations will be joined. As we view the matter, God has never had but one church in the world, and never will have but one, to which all true believers, and redeemed sinners will belong from Adam down through eternal ages.

The restoration, and conversion, and exaltation of the seed of Abraham, in the manner described in the prophets, will be necessary to a fulfillment of the ancient promise. God promised to give to Abraham and his seed the land of Canaan, for an everlasting possession. And now, what will become of this promise, if his seed are forever to be exiled from the land given them?

But take all these predictions according to their obvious import, and every thing is made plain. Not one iota of God's word shall fail. All this may be humbling to the haughty Gentile in his contempt and oppression of the now despised Jew; but the day will come when the lofty looks of man shall be humbled, and the haughtiness of man shall be bowed down, and the Lord alone be exalted.—Isaiah 2: 10–17.

The prophet Ezekiel, from the fortieth chapter to the end of his book, foretells the restoration of the Jews, the rebuilding of Jerusalem, and the reëstablishment of the worship of the Lord, in connection with the temple then to be erected, with great minuteness and particularity. That which he has here described has manifestly never been fulfilled. It must, then, be future. Millennarians suppose that all that is here predicted will, in the manner and form intended, be yet accomplished, and that the great design of the temple services and sacrifices there instituted, will be retrospective, and intended to keep before the minds of the successive generations of redeemed men, that they owe their salvation entirely to Christ, who died on Calvary that they might live.

It is a settled fact in revelation, that there remaineth no more sacrifice for sin; that, by one offering, Christ hath perfected forever them that are sanctified. The world will never need any other sacrifice, and no new atonement will ever be made. Now, did millennarians ever so interpret the prophecies as to teach that there would be, it would be certain proof that they were wrong. But a sacrifice instituted as an atonement, and a sacrifice instituted as a commemorative ordinance, as was the Passover, and to answer the same or a similar purpose as the Lord's Supper, are very different things. Now, it is supposed that these sacrifices and offerings predicted by Ezekiel, will be entirely commemorative, and will look back to Calvary as the Lord's Supper does now. Will all this be unreasonable and absurd? Let us suppose for a moment, that the world is entirely redeemed from sin and the curse, and that the generations of men, hence, are sanctified from the womb, and grow up as plants of righteousness in the garden of the Lord, to be transplanted to heaven in God's own time and way.

Now, all these generations, through countless ages, will owe their salvation to Christ. Should the inquiry be made for or amid the redeemed and sanctified nations, Why is it that we are sinless and grow up and ripen for higher glory, without being called, as our fathers were in former ages, to contend with temptation, and corruption, and death? the answer will be, Jesus died, and as the purchase of his death, and the travail of his soul, we inherit these exalted and eternal blessings.

And now, as the kingdom of God is a kingdom of means, is it unreasonable to suppose that the Lord will appoint some appropriate service, which, in its nature, shall be adapted to remind them, and impressively affect them with this great truth? And what could be more appropriate or impressive than a reinstitution, for another purpose, of those sacrifices which, before the first advent of our Lord, typified his atonement? Will there not be an impressive adaptation in these, to remind the nations, as they shall go up to Jerusalem to worship, from generation to generation, that all their blessings flow to them by the Cross? And thus, as believers in former ages, were directed by their sacrifices to an atoning sacrifice which was to be offered, so these, in the future economy, will point the redeemed on earth back to that same sacrifice already offered, once for all. And thus the past and the future will be concentrated at one point, and in one only Saviour.

Viewed in this aspect, should all that the prophets have foretold be literally fulfilled, there would, to my mind, be in the arrangement something inexpressibly beautiful and grand, worthy of God, and adapted to the circumstances of a world made holy through the atonement of Jesus.

Looking at the subject in this light, no truth, or doctrine, or principle, clearly revealed in the scripture, is denied, nor is anything detracted from its significance; but a more ample, and enlarged, and extended view is given to the whole scheme of redeeming love.

It has been thought absurd by some, that all nations should literally go up to Jerusalem to worship the Lord, from one month to another, and from year to year. But these predictions would all be fully complied with, were the nations to go up simply by their representatives, just as the United States assemble in Congress by their representatives. And then who can tell what new modes of travel may be in use in the future? Had it been told to our fathers, a few years ago, that the time would come when men would travel through the country by steam, at the rate of fifty or sixty miles an hour, and across the Atlantic in nine or ten days, and transmit intelligence around the world in an instant of time, no one would have believed it. But think you that we have reached the utmost limit of improvement? It is possible, in view of the past, that such improvements may yet be made, that all that is predicted about going up to Jerusalem to worship from one new moon to another, may be pleasantly and joyfully accomplished, and to a much larger extent than we can now conceive. At any rate, we know that God can do, or cause to be done, all that he has promised, and none can hinder.

It is often objected to the restoration of the Jews to their own land, and to the fulfillment of the prophecies in the manner and form presented, that there will be no use in it all.

There might not be any particular use in their restoration and reorganization as a nation devoted to God, on some theories, but according to the millennarian view there will be great and glorious results to be accomplished.

1. What a sublime demonstration it will furnish to the world and the universe of the everlasting faithfulness of God, and how it will tend to sustain the faith of the redeemed, through eternal ages! God has shown his faithfulness in the preservation of Israel as a distinct people to the present time, and when in future ages he shall magnify his Word in the conversion of all Israel, and in giving them the land of promise, as an everlasting possession, and cause the nations of earth to be eternally blessed through the seed of Abraham, what an affecting exhibition it will be to angels and men, of the certainty and stability of any covenant which God may make.

And may not the redeemed with Christ, need some such monument of the faithfulness of God, to assure them of the eternity of their perfection and blessedness?

When the saved are put in possession of their eternal reward, how will they know that it will never, in any way, be wrested from them? With the examples before them, that angels once holy and happy fell, and that man in innocence trangressed, how can they know that they will not, at some point in their career, be tempted to sin, and perish? But they cannot. Why? Because God has promised them eternal life. He who cannot lie, has said, "They shall never perish," and his word cannot fail. Now, in regard to the saved, it will be their unwavering faith in these promises of God, which will give them the assurance that no sin or ruin shall ever sweep over them. And as God strengthens the faith of his people by means, may it not be necessary that their faith should be sustained unshaken, by some living, practical, and eternal demonstration of his faithfulness in the fulfillment of his word?

And will not such a demonstration be furnished in a restored world, in the literal fulfillment of all the ancient promises to the seed of Abraham, as through illimitable ages they shall multiply, in their own land, and having fulfilled their destiny on earth, shall, by transfiguration, go up to mingle in higher scenes among the glorified? Can it be conceived that the Lord could give a more practical and sublime exhibition of his faithfulness and love to the redeemed, or a stronger assurance that nothing should ever fail to them of all that he had promised, than in Israel's predicted exaltation and glory?

We make no positive declarations on points not clearly revealed, but the suggestions are in accordance with facts, and may prove a glorious reality in the world to come. But,

2. For ought we know, the restoration of the Jews to their own land, converted and sanctified, as the great central point of the redeemed church, around which the converted nations shall be gathered, as participants in the river of life, which shall flow from the throne of God, may be the very best arrangement of eternal wisdom and love, to unite all the fami-

lies of earth in indissoluble bonds of brotherhood and interest, and in perfecting the great scheme of salvation. Can we deny that this may be so? And though the utility of the arrangement may not now appear to all, shall we question the wisdom of God, or arraign his counsels at the bar of human reason, and short-sighted ignorance? Better for us to wait, under the assurance that what we know not now, we shall know hereafter. The vision which God has given is certain, and all his purposes will be fulfilled in their time.

"Behold the measure of the promise fill'd;
See Salem built, the labor of a God!
Bright as a sun the sacred city shines;
All kingdoms and all princes of the earth
Flock to that light; the glory of all lands
Flows into her; unbounded is her joy,
And endless her increase. Thy rams are there,
Nebaioth, and the flocks of Kedar there:
The looms of Ormus, and the mines of Ind,
And Saba's spicy groves, pay tribute there.
Praise is in all her gates; upon her walls,
And in her streets, and in her spacious courts,
Is heard salvation. Eastern Java there
Kneels with the native of the farthest west;
And Ethiopia spreads abroad the hand,
And worships. Her report has travel'd forth
Into all lands. From every clime they come
To see thy beauty, and to share thy joy,
O Sion! an assembly such as earth
Saw never, such as Heaven stoops down to see."

Chapter Seventh.

THE JUDGMENT DAY.

It is clearly revealed in scripture, that God "hath appointed a day, in which he will judge the world in righteousness, by that man whom he hath ordained, whereof he hath given assurance unto all men, in that he hath raised him from the dead." In this great and solemn transaction all are concerned; "for we must all appear before the judgment seat of Christ, that every one may receive the things done in the body, according to that he hath done, whether it be good or bad." These, and kindred scriptures, are to be received in their full and literal integrity, and any system of doctrine, professedly derived from the Bible, which would deny their truth or explain them to mean something else, cannot be true.

But to give these predictions of a judgment to come their full and consistent import, must we necessarily understand the day of judgment to mean simply a day of twelve or twenty-four hours? and must we restrict the great Judge to this contracted period, and believe that all those great and fearful acts which are to be accomplished at that day, and the judgment of every individual, with every secret thing, are to be circumscribed within one diurnal revolution? Suppose we should understand the day of judgment to denote a definite and fixed time of judgment, comprehending a period of time sufficiently long to accomplish in orderly and impressive succession, all that God has said that he will do on that day, would it be a denial of the great truth that we must all appear before the judgment seat of Christ?

The scriptures furnish many examples which show that a day, in the language of God, is frequently employed to represent an indefinite or definite period of time, of longer or shorter duration to be determined by the connection. Thus, Eccl. 7 : 14. "In the day of prosperity be joyful; but in the day of adversity consider: God also has set the one over against the other, to the end that man should find nothing after him." Here, day is used to denote the time, however long or short, during which posperity is enjoyed, or adversity suffered.

Is. 63 : 4. "For the day of vengeance is in my heart, and the year of my redeemed is come." Ez. 7 : 7. "The morning is come upon thee, O thou that dwellest in the land : the time is come, the day of trouble is near."

Nahum 1 : 7. "The Lord is good, a strong hold in the day of trouble." In these, and numerous other passages, the word day denotes a period of time indefinite in duration.

John 9 : 4. "I must work the works of him that sent me, while it is day: the night cometh when no man can work."

Here, it stands for the whole period of the Saviour's life on earth, and accordingly it is common to call every man's life his day.—Heb. 3 : 7, 8. "Wherefore, as the Holy Ghost saith, To-day if ye will hear his voice, Harden not your hearts, as in the provocation, in the day of temptation in the wilderness: When your fathers tempted me, proved me, and saw my works forty years." In this passage the day of temptation is explained to mean forty years. And then immediately afterward we have it employed to represent the season of grace, however long it may be: "While it is said, To-day if ye will hear his voice, harden not your hearts, as in the provocation."

These passages might be indefinitely multiplied, in which the word day is used to denote a term of trouble or blessing, without limiting the duration. And this use of the word is in accordance with all the usages of common life.

No violence is then done to the use of language, or to scripture, when the day of judgment is understood to represent, not a period of twenty-four hours, but a time of judgment fixed in the purpose of God, and embracing a period long enough to accomplish all that God has said he will do. In fact, it is absolutely necessary that we should give this extended import to the day of judgment; for how can every individual give an account of himself to God, and every work and every secret thing be brought into judgment, of all the vast millions of men who have ever lived, in one short day? And why should the Infinite be in a hurry? Is there not stretching on beyond the utmost limits of time, an unending eternity?

And may not the Great Judge take time enough to spread out before a finite universe, the grounds of his judgments and the mysteries of providence, so as to produce an effect most impressive and instructive, upon principalities and powers, who shall be spectators of the scene?

Accordingly, though the scriptures teach that God has appointed a day of judgment, yet, should they inform us in other places that this day denoted a hundred or a thousand years there would be no contradiction in the statements.

And now, at this great period, this great day of God Almighty, when he will judge angels and men, should he judge best in his wisdom, to divide the human family into three bands, and then proceed to judge each in their order, according to their works, and at such intervals as he might determine, it would still be true that all would appear before the Judgment Seat of Christ, and at the day of judgment.

In accordance with these views, millennarians hold, as we understand them, that there will be two great acts or times of judgment corresponding to the two resurrections described, and confirmed in a previous chapter; and these will both be included within the period denoted by the judgment day.

At the appearing of our Lord, he will first judge the quick or the living, and the dead, who are raised up at that time; and then at the close of the thousand years, he will raise and judge the wicked dead, with the devil and his angels. These, with intermediate and attending events, will be considered in order.

1. According to scripture, when Christ comes, he will judge and reward his servants, raised and glorified, and in intimate connection with them, he will judge among the living nations, and will consume Antichrist, and all who will not that he should reign over them. It would be vain for finite man to describe the order which these judgments will take except as they are revealed; but the great facts in the case, and the persons who are to be judged, at his appearing and kingdom, are definitely recorded.

Rev. 11: 15–19. "The sounding of the seventh angel, announces, that the kingdoms of this world are become the kingdoms of our Lord, and of his Christ; and he shall reign forever and ever." But this is not the only thing proclaimed, at the ushering in of that glorious era: for it is immediately added: "And the four and twenty Elders, which sat before God on their seats, fell upon their faces and worshipped God, saying, We give thee thanks, O Lord God Almighty, which art, and wast, and art to come; because thou hast taken to thee thy great power, and hast reigned.

"And the nations were angry, and thy wrath is come, and the time of the dead, that they should be judged." *What dead?* It is immediately explained. "And that thou shouldst give reward unto thy servants the prophets, and to the saints, and them that fear thy name, small and great, and shouldst destroy them which destroy the earth."

Here we are definitely informed, that at the time the kingdoms of this world become the kingdoms of our Lord, the saints of God, small and great, will be rewarded, and that at the same time also there will be angry nations, who will not that the Saviour should reign over them, who will be judged and destroyed from the earth, as were the Antediluvians, and the Sodomites of old.

The same truth is brought to view in the parable of the Nobleman.—Luke 19 : 11–27. In this parable, our Lord is represented, as calling together his servants, on his return to earth, and reckoning with them, and rewarding them with offices in his kingdom, according to their fidelity in improving the pounds committed to their care. But there were those not numbered among his servants, who said, we will not have this man to reign over us. And in regard to these, he will say, " But those, mine enemies, which would not that I should reign over them, bring them hither and slay them before me." The representations of this parable are most strikingly in harmony with the view of the judgment day here advocated.

The prophecy contained in the second Psalm, also indicates a vast destruction of some who will not be reconciled to Christ the Son.

" Ask of me, and I will give the the heathen," or the Gentile nations " for thine inheritance, and the uttermost parts of the earth for thy possession." What then? All converted and saved? Read. " Thou shalt rule over them with a rod of iron: thou shalt dash them in pieces like a potter's vessel. Be wise now, therefore, O ye kings: be instructed ye judges of the earth. Serve the Lord with fear, and rejoice with trembling. Kiss the Son, lest he be angry, and ye perish from the way, when his wrath is kindled but a little. Blessed are all they that put their trust in him."

At this period, then, when the Gentile nations shall be given to the Son, there will be those who will not be reconciled to him, and whom it will be necessary by judgments, to remove from the earth, that it may be redeemed from sin. And then, in regard to others, it is said:

"And he shall judge among the nations, and shall rebuke strong nations afar off, and they shall beat their swords into plough-shares, and their spears into pruning-hooks; nation shall not lift up sword against nation, neither shall they learn war any more."

The same fearful judgment of the angered and apostate living nations, is described in Rev. 19: 11–21. "And I saw heaven opened, and behold, a white horse; and he that sat upon him was called Faithful and True, and in righteousness doth he *judge* and make war. His eyes were as a flame of fire, and on his head were many crowns; and he had a name written, that no man knew but himself. And he was clothed in a vesture dipped in blood: and his name is called, The Word of God.

"And the armies which were in heaven followed him upon white horses, clothed in fine linen, white and clean. And out of his mouth goeth a sharp tow-edged sword, that with it he should smite the nations: And he shall rule them with a rod of iron." Ps. 2: 9. "And he treadeth the wine-press of the fierceness and wrath of Almighty God."

"And hath on his vesture and on his thigh, a name written, KING OF KINGS, AND LORD OF LORDS.

"And I saw an angel standing in the sun; and he cried with a loud voice, saying, to all the fowls that fly in the midst of heaven, Come, and gather yourselves together unto the supper of the great God; that ye may eat the flesh of kings, and the flesh of captains, and the flesh of mighty men, and the flesh of horses, and of them that sit on them, and the flesh of all men, both free and bond, both small and great.

"And I saw the beast, and the kings of the earth, and

their armies, gathered together to make war against him that sat on the horse, and against his army.

"And the beast was taken, and with him the false prophet, that wrought miracles before him, with which he deceived them that had received the mark of the beast, and them that worshipped his image. These were both cast alive into a lake burning with fire and brimstone.

"And the remnant were slain with the sword of him that sat upon the horse, which sword proceeded out of his mouth: and all the fowls were filled with their flesh."

Now, no one supposes that all this is to be taken in a literal sense. The language is undoubtedly symbolical; but who can doubt that a fearful destruction is here foretold, among those nations who arraign themselves against the King of kings, and who will not that he should reign over them? Is not here a terrific judgment described, over apostates and rebels, when Babylon shall come in remembrance, and fall with violence?

And the fact here specified, that he shall rule them with a rod of iron, identifies those spoken of with the Gentile nations, described in Psalms 2: 9, who will not be reconciled to the Son, and whom he will rule with a rod of iron, and break in pieces like a potter's vessel.

The summoning, too, of all the fowls of heaven to the feast of the great God, representing a scene which has often followed the slaughter of battle, *seems* to identify the destruction here predicted, with the destruction of Gog and Magog, described in Ezekiel 38 and 39, in which the same summons is sent to birds and beasts, to come to the great sacrifice which will be made by their slaughter. By a reference to chapter 14: 6–20, we find that the same terrible judgment among the nations, and especially among the apostate nations represented by Babylon, the mother of harlots, are associated with the flying of the angel through mid-heaven, having the everlasting gospel to preach unto them that dwell on the earth, and also with the coming of the Son of Man in the clouds of heaven.

Verses 14–20. "And I looked and beheld a white cloud, and upon the cloud one sat like unto the Son of Man, having on his head a golden crown, and in his hand a sharp sickle.

"And another angel came out of the temple, crying with a loud voice to him that sat on the cloud, Thrust in thy sickle and reap: for the time is come for thee to reap: for the harvest of the earth is ripe.

"And he that sat on the cloud thrust in his sickle on the earth; and the earth was reaped.

"And another angel came out of the temple which is in heaven, he also having a sharp sickle.

"And another angel came out from the altar which had power over fire; and he cried with a loud cry to him that had the sharp sickle, saying, Thrust in thy sharp sickle, and gather the clusters of the vine of the earth; for her grapes are fully ripe. And the angel thrust in his sickle into the earth, and gathered the vine of the earth, and cast it into the great wine press of the wrath of God. And the wine-press was trodden without the city, and blood came out of the wine-press, even unto the horses' bridles, by the space of a thousand and six hundred furlongs."

The symbols here employed are clearly of fearful import, and denote some terrible judgments, bloody and destructive, which will yet come upon the nations designated. And they are manifestly future, from the fact that they are associated with, and immediately follow the publishing of the gospel to the nations of earth, and are connected with the coming of one like the Son of Man upon a cloud, the symbol of our Lord's appearing.

And we are not left in doubt in regard to those who are comprehended in these vast destructions. There is one infallible sign given, with which God points his finger, and says, these are the people.

Rev. 16: 5-7. "And I heard the angel of the waters say, Thou art righteous, O Lord, which art, and wast, and shalt be, because thou hast judged thus, For they have shed the blood of saints and prophets, and thou hast given them blood to drink; for they are worthy."—18: 24. "And in her was found the blood of prophets, and of saints, and of all that were slain upon the earth."

Can there be any doubt, then, in regard to the powers meant in these fearful predictions? And do not all these point to the same angered nations mentioned in chapter eleventh, where it is said, that when God shall judge the righteous dead, and give reward unto his servants small and great, he will destroy those who have destroyed the earth, by their apostasies and persecutions?

Now, how exactly do all these prophetic representations correspond to the fact foretold by the apostle, that the Man of Sin is to be consumed with the spirit of Christ's mouth, and destroyed with the brightness of his coming?—and with the prophecy in Daniel, that the Little Horn is to be judged at the coming of the Son of Man in the clouds of heaven to receive the dominion of earth?—and also, with the gathering of the tares out from among the wheat at the end of the dispensation?

Let not the reader be shocked at these revelations of future destruction to apostate, persecuting and blood-stained nations, as though it would be derogatory to the character of God, and the benevolence of Jesus, thus to deal with nations, and providentially to suffer the blood of those to be shed, who have wickedly shed the blood of the saints. What is here threatened is no more than has repeatedly been inflicted in the fearful judgments of the past. The old world was destroyed with a flood. Sodom and Gomorrah with fire and brimstone, and mighty nations denounced for their sins in prophecy have perished from earth. May not God yet carry on this work of judgment, and sweep other nations, equally corrupt, from the world without dishonoring his justice or benevolence? It is possible for nations, as well as individuals, to become so corrupt, morally and physically, that their removal from earth, by war, pestilence or famine, would not only be just, but an act of highest benevolence to the living. It is recorded in scripture that God will render to men as they have rendered to others, and accordingly we find it fearfully illustrated in history, that they who have reared their thrones amid the carnage of slaughtered nations, have, in process of time, been overturned in blood, and have perished amid the desolations of war.

So God has determined that they who have shed the blood of the saints, shall have blood in return. By letting loose upon them their enemies, and turning back upon them the desolations of war, they will reap that which they have sown.

In the prophets are numerous and fearful warnings to the nations, and to the wicked generally, in view of this great day of reckoning that is coming. Joel says, 3: 9–18:

"Proclaim ye this among the Gentiles: Prepare war, wake up the mighty men, let all the men of war draw near; let them come up: Beat your plough-shares into swords, and your pruning-hooks into spears; let the weak say, I am strong. Assemble yourselves, and come, all ye Gentiles, and gather yourselves together round about: thither cause the mighty ones to come down, O Lord.

"Let the heathen be wakened and come up to the valley of Jehoshaphat, for there will I sit to judge all the heathen round about. Put ye in the sickle for the harvest is ripe." See Rev. 19: "Come, get you down, for the press is full, the fats overflow, for their wickedness is great. Multitudes,

multitudes in the valley of decision; for the day of the Lord is near in the valley of decision. The sun and the moon shall be darkened, and the stars shall withdraw their shining," that is, the reigning and oppressive powers of earth shall be overthrown, the heavenly bodies here standing as symbols for them.

"The Lord shall rear out of Zion, and utter his voice from Jerusalem; and the heavens and the earth shall shake; but the Lord will be the hope of his people, and the strength of the children of Israel. So shall ye know that I am the Lord your God dwelling in Zion, my holy mountain: then shall Jerusalem be holy, and there shall no strangers pass through her any more. And it shall come to pass in that day, that the mountains shall drop new wine, and the hills shall flow with milk, and all the rivers of Judah shall flow with waters, and a fountain shall come forth of the house of the Lord, and shall water the valley of Shittim."

How can we avoid the conviction that there is a fearful day of reckoning and judgment coming on the nations, in which they will be broken to pieces as a potter's vessel, and consumed with terrible destructions? While, therefore, a slumbering world is crying, peace, peace, God is sounding an alarm in all his holy mountain, and admonishing the nations to be wise and tremble, and kiss the Son. The day of wrath is coming, it is hastening on apace, when all who have shed the blood of saints, will have blood in return, and when all who will not that Christ should reign over them will be cut off from earth, to take their places at a more remote judgment with Sodom and Gomorrah.

A careful comparison of these various predictions will show that they are all associated and identified with the coming of our Lord, the destruction of Antichrist, the sanctification and restoration of Jerusalem, and the conversion of the world.

When they occur, the destruction of these enemies of Christ and his people will, no doubt, be seen to be in great mercy to the world. It is possible, as before observed, for nations and individuals to become so wicked and corrupt, that God cannot consistently with his government save them, and their removal from earth will be in great mercy to the living, as was the destruction of the old world, and Sodom and Gomorrah. To cleanse the world and make it an abode of righteousness, their removal will be necessary. And would not this be better than to suffer them to remain here to perpetuate their wickedness and desolations?

But when these judgments come, they will not be universally inflicted; for Judah shall then be saved, and Jerusalem shall dwell safely, and among all the nations there will be salvation.

Even in the Apocalyptic Babylon, fallen and ruined, and doomed to destruction, God will have a people whom he will save in the day when she shall receive the reward of her wickedness.—Rev. 18: 4. "And I heard another voice from heaven, saying, Come out of her my people, that ye be not partakers of her sins, and that ye receive not of her plagues."

There will be a sifting then among the nations, and a just and benevolent discrimination; for God will not suffer one who has given a cup of water in his name to lose his reward.

It is believed by millennarians, that to this judgment among the nations, and this discrimination which will be made at that time, by the Great Judge, when he thall sit upon the throne of his glory, is to be referred the parable of the sheep and goats, in the twenty-fifth of Matthew.

But, should the reader dispute this, and maintain that it can only have reference to the last judgment, it would not affect the arguments already presented, or disprove the doctrines advanced.

The great principles of justice and reward laid down in this parable, will, no doubt, characterize all the judgments of God; but there is a most striking manifestation of millennarian views in this parable. The parable does not intimate that there are any included in the judgment at that time but the living nations.

There is nothing said about any among those then judged, who are raised from the dead. It is a very different thing from the judgment described in Rev. 20: 12, where John saw the dead, small and great, stand before God, and when the sea and hell are represented as giving up the dead that are in them, in order to judgment.

It is only the living nations, who are assembled before him in this parable, and among whom he will judge and discriminate, and only these, who would not that he should reign over them, are destroyed. And he will separate them one from another as a shepherd divideth his sheep from the goats. And to those who have not persecuted and oppressed his people, but who have shown kindness to them, and succored them in time of need, or who have given to any a cup of cold water because they belonged to Christ, he will say, "Come, ye blessed of my Father, inherit the kingdom, this glorious kingdom now set up, prepared for such as you, from the foundation of the world, for I was an hungered and ye gave me meat, &c."

Upon such the gift of immortality will then be conferred, the curse of death will never come upon them. Having fulfilled their lot and time on earth, they will be transfigured to glory without experiencing death, as was Enoch and Elijah in former times, and as were the living saints at the resurrection of the holy dead.

The removal of the curse of death from our world is foretold by the prophets, and is symbolized in the tree of life in the new Jerusalem, the leaves of which are for the healing of the nations in the flesh.

Now, the fact that only those in this parable are rewarded, who have fed, and clothed, and visited the brethren of Christ in tribulation, shows that it is not a universal judgment here described, for tens of thousands of the saved never had the opportunity, or the ability, to do the things here mentioned, as is the case with the infant race and others.

We think, then, the position is clearly sustained, that when Christ comes he will first judge and reward his saints, and that at, or in connection with the same time, he will judge the living nations, and destroy Antichrist—those who have shed the blood of his saints, and who have destroyed the earth, by their oppressions and corruptions.

Probably most of these destructions will be effected in the Providence of God, as in former times, by wars and revolutions, and fearful collisions; but it is clear, from scripture, that the last act of crowning justice and judgment upon earth, will be by fire—even by that last awful conflagration described by Peter, 2 Epistle 3: 9.

In reference to this, Malachi says, 4: 1. "For behold, the day cometh that shall burn as an oven; and all the proud, yea, all that do wickedly, shall be stubble; and the day that cometh shall burn them up, saith the Lord of hosts, that it shall leave them neither root nor branch. But unto you that fear my name, shall the sun of righteousness arise with healing in his wings; and ye shall go forth, and grow up as calves of the stall. And ye shall tread down the wicked; for they shall be ashes under the soles of your feet, in the day that I shall do this, saith the Lord of hosts."

The description of Peter is equally vivid and awful. "But the heavens and the earth which are now, by the same word are kept in store reserved unto fire against the day of judgment and perdition of ungodly men. But the day of the

Lord will come as a thief in the night; in the which the heavens shall pass away with a great noise, and the elements shall melt with fervent heat, and the earth also, and the works that are therein, shall be burned up.

"Seeing, then, that all these things shall be dissolved, what manner of persons ought ye to be in all holy conversation and godliness. Looking for and hasting unto the coming of the day of God, wherein the heavens being on fire, shall be dissolved, and the elements shall melt with fervent heat.

"Nevertheless, we, according to his promise, look not for annihilation, but for new heavens and a new earth, wherein dwelleth righteousness." Some have regarded this as a prediction of the entire destruction and annihilation of the material world.

But the scriptures must be consistent with themselves, and any exposition which brings one part in contradiction to another cannot be true. There are various scriptures which show that nothing like an entire destruction or an annihilation of the material world is intended in these predictions.

1. It is absolutely and unconditionally affirmed that this world is to abide forever.

Eccl. 1: 4. "One generation passeth away, and another generation cometh; *but the earth abideth forever.*" Psalms 105: 5.—"Who laid the foundations of the earth, that it should not be *removed forever.*" It cannot therefore be taught that the earth is at any time to be annihilated without contradicting these clear and positive annunciations.

2. It is certain that by the conflagration foretold by Peter nothing like an entire destruction can be meant; because it is to be followed, not by another, but by a new heaven and a new earth, in which righteous people shall dwell. And this will be the fulfillment of a prophecy of Isaiah, 65: 17. And now if we turn to this promise, we shall find that in

this new heavens and earth, Jerusalem is to be made a rejoicing, and her people a joy—that animals shall exist, the wolf and the lamb feed together, and the lion eat straw with the bullock.

3. The prophets repeatedly affirm and reaffirm in the most formal and solemn manner, that when the dominion of Jesus Christ is perfectly established over this world, it shall exist forever, and that of the increase of his government upon the throne of David there shall positively be no end. But if the earth is literally to be burned up and annihilated, in the course of a few thousand years, as some maintain, then Christ's kingdom on earth will not be everlasting, and to the increase of his government on the throne of David there will be an end. Hence it is certain that no such thing as an entire destruction of the material world and the race of man on earth can be intended by the apostle. To give a limited meaning to the words, forever and everlasting, as applied to the duration of the earth, and the perpetuity of Christ's kingdom in the earth, would effectually destroy the argument derived from these terms for the endless perpetuity of happiness and misery in the world to come.

4. The fact that it is a destruction produced by fire, shows that it cannot mean annihilation. It is a well-established principle in philosophy that fire cannot annihilate a single particle of matter upon which it acts. It can only change its form and chemical combinations. As, therefore, the nature of an effect must correspond to the nature of the cause which produces it, it is certain that the world and every particle of which it is composed must remain here after the conflagration.

5. The discoveries of astronomy furnish a strong argument for the stability and perpetuity of the earth, and the whole material universe through infinite ages.

"The conjecture of Sir W. Herschell, near seventy years

ago, is believed to be verified, that our sun is changing its position in relation to the stars, by a motion round a central orb, like that of its own planets round itself; that it advances along the line of its orbit more than 30,000,000 of miles a year, and that the circuit on which it moves is so immense that 1,800,000 of our years would be comprised in the period of a single revolution."

Now, is it reasonable to suppose that our earth will be, or may be blotted out of existence, before the system of which it is a part has performed one of these mighty revolutions? Does not its movement on such a line, around a grand central orb, furnish adequate ground for the inference that it is to complete and repeat that revolution, as certainly as it was the design of the Creator that our earth should perform unnumbered revolutions round the sun?

In view of the sublime movements and immensity of the material universe, and in consideration of the fact that it is in the glory of these heavens, that the glory of God is manifested and declared to created beings, how unreasonable the idea that the bosom of destruction is to sweep over all these handiworks of God, and that the whole universe is to be lighted up into one grand funeral pile, to waste in utter nothingness. How much more consistent the idea that the Saviour shall forever rejoice in this habitable world, and preserve it to eternal ages, as a monument of redeeming love, in which he will multiply his seed without end.

6. It is evident that the apostle Peter does not predict anything like a destruction of the material world, from the fact that it is to be a destruction of a corresponding nature to that produced by the waters of the deluge.

Of the scoffers who, he predicted, would arise in the last days, denying the second literal coming of our Lord, he says, "For this they willingly are ignorant of, that by the word of God the heavens were of old, and the earth standing out of the water and in the water: whereby the world that then was, being overflowed with water perished: but the heavens and the earth which are now, by the same word are kept in store, reserved unto fire against the day of judgment and perdition of ungodly men."

Now, here is a comparison instituted, showing us, that as the earth perished once by water, so in a similar manner, and for the same reason will it, at some future time, perish by fire. But in what sense did the earth perish by water? Was one particle of matter annihilated? Did not the earth still remain after the flood, with its mountains and valleys, its oceans and rivers, and with its Ararat, upon which the ark rested? Did anything in fact perish, except that for which the flood was sent, the destruction of man, and such animals as could not live in or upon water? It is clear that the material world did not perish by the flood—it was only the world of men and such other living things as God designed. The flood was designed for the perdition of ungodly men; and for the same reason will be commissioned the fires of the last conflagration: for, says the apostle, "The heavens and earth which are now reserved unto fire, against the day of judgment and perdition of ungodly men." And hence—

7. It may be remarked, that as the design of God, in this fire, is the perdition or destruction of ungodly men from the earth, as was the flood, and as no others are named among the things which are to perish, but ungodly men and their works, the prediction does not assert or imply the entire dissolution and destruction of the material earth. We might just as logically argue, that because the old world being overflowed with water, perished, therefore it was actually all dissolved and annihilated, as to argue that because the heavens, or the atmosphere and the earth are to be subjected

to the action, in some sense, of fire, that therefore the whole is to be blotted out.

As the fire is designed for the perdition of ungodly men and their works, it will have accomplished its whole mission when these ends are effected. But—

8. The description of the apostle shows that the predicted fire is to be principally or wholly in the atmosphere, and is to act only on the surface of the earth, for the purposes which it is to accomplish. He says, "But the day of the Lord will come as a thief in the night: in the which, the heavens," that is the atmosphere, "shall pass," or rush "with a great noise, and the elements shall melt with fervent heat, the earth also, and the works therein, shall be burned," that is, by being in contact with the electrical or other fires enkindled in the air.

Again he says, "Looking for, and hasting unto the coming of the day of God, wherein the heavens being on fire shall be dissolved, and the elements shall melt with fervent heat." Surely, there is no prediction of an annihilation here. It is to be the atmosphere that is to be the subject and scene of the fire. "The earth is to be burned by the contact of the kindled air with its surface, not by the enkindling of its whole mass. This is indicated by the statement that the works on it, that is, the works of men are to be burned." And all this is rendered certain, from the fact already presented, that there is immediately to be a new heavens, and a new earth, "and their newness is to consist in their renovation; the atmosphere, instead of pestilential, is to become congenial to life; the earth, instead of being blighted with sterility, and overrun with thorns, is to become fruitful. Wildernesses are to bud and blossom as the rose, and deserts smile with verdure and plenty. And in this new heavens and earth, Jerusalem is to become a rejoicing, and her people a joy."—Is. 65: 17.

The great design of this fire, as recorded by the apostle,

and by Malachi, chapter 4, is to remove the incorrigibly wicked from the earth, those who will not that the Lord should reign over them, and to convert our world into an abode of righteousness. It will be the great crowning act of God's judgment among the living nations, when the wicked will be removed, to appear at the resurrection of the wicked and their final judgment, at the close of the millennium.

The great difficulty in regard to this subject, in the minds of some, is this ;—if men, and nations, and animals, are to live upon the earth after the conflagration, as the prophets teach, how can they, or are they to be preserved alive amid the flaming fires of this great day? For one, I answer, I do not know ; but this I do know, that he who knew how to preserve man and beast, when the old world perished by water, who could save Lot from a burning Sodom, and Shadrach, Mesheck, and Abednego, from the flames of the furnace into which they were cast, can easily save all men and animals that he has purposed. And the fact that he has not revealed how he will do it, is no proof that he cannot, or will not. Suppose when God revealed the great fact that he would destroy the earth with a flood, but yet would save one family, and a sufficient number of animals to repeople and replenish the world, he had designedly withheld the information, as to the manner in which he would save them, could it have been confidently argued, that the facts, as predicted, could not take place, because there was no way revealed, in which any could be saved from the devouring elements?

Neither can it now be rationally objected that men and animals cannot live on the earth after the fires predicted, because the mode of preservation is not disclosed.

The fact is, we know too little of the precise nature of the conflagration, or how it will proceed, or how long it will last, or whether it will be universal at the same time, to raise many objections on this score.

If God has said, there shall be a new heavens and a new earth, in which Jerusalem shall be rebuilt, and in which nations and animals shall exist, as described in Isaiah 65 : 17–25, then, undoubtedly, all will be fulfilled.

The Almighty, whose power none can resist, could easily collect all he intended to save in some prepared refuge or hiding place, around and above which the lightnings might play in fearful terror, and the elements burn with resistless energy and leave them unharmed. And it is not improbable that it is to these secret hiding places, which God will provide for man and beast, that reference is made in Isaiah 26 : 20, 21, where God says, "Come, my people, enter thou into thy chambers, and shut thy doors about thee : hide thyself, as it were for a little moment, until the indignation be overpast. For behold, the Lord cometh out of his place to punish the inhabitants of the earth for their iniquity : the earth also shall disclose her blood, and shall no more cover her slain."

From the connection in which these words stand, and from the fact that they refer to a final and thorough cleansing of the earth from all violence and blood, it seems that they were designed to point to those chambers of refuge and safety which God will prepare, as he did the ark for Noah, in which his people, being warned, will betake themselves from the storms of fire and destruction which will rage without. None will have cause to fear in this great day, but the ungodly, who yield not to Jesus.

And now, is it not an exceedingly delightful thought, that this world is never to be destroyed, but is to stand a monument of redeeming power and love through eternal ages ? Can we ever forget the home of our childhood, the world whence commenced our immortal existence, in which Jesus died, where we were renewed by the Spirit and trained for immortal glories, and which has been the theatre of such wonderous scenes?

O, as by permission, we may range this glorious universe, and take our fill of joy amid the heaven of heavens, will it not be pleasant sometimes to come back to earth, and visit the spots around which cluster memories which can never be erased? I doubt not the fires of the last conflagration will leave the localities of earth so unchanged, that familiar and cherished spots may be still to the holy associated with all that is interesting and affecting.

And now, reader, as this is manifestly not unscriptural, is it an unworthy, a degrading, and corrupting view of the subject? Is it indulging in groveling sensualities? And is it in any way adapted to diminish from the bright anticipations of future glory revealed in the scriptures?

Having now considered the judgment of the raised and transfigured saints, and of the living nations on earth, at the commencement of the thousand years, we will pass over the millennium, during all which time the Lord will judge among the redeemed nations, in righteousness, and truth, and love, and come down to the resurrection and judgment of the wicked who will then be raised.

Satan, we are assured, is to be bound a thousand years, and when the thousand years are expired, he is to be loosed out of his prison. Simultaneously with the loosing of Satan, all those who have no part in the first resurrection are raised up from the dead,—so it is recorded, "And the rest of the dead lived not again until the thousand years were finished;" and this certainly implies that they will live again upon earth at that time. The design of the loosing of Satan at this time, and the resurrection of the wicked, is in order to the last scenes and acts of judgment. And accordingly, the Revelator immediately adds: "And I saw the dead, small and great, stand before God; and the books were opened: and another book was opened, which is the book of life: and the dead were judged out of those things which are written in the books, according to their works. And the sea gave up the dead which were in it, and death and hell delivered up the dead which were in them: and they were judged, every man according to their works. And death and hell were cast into the lake of fire. This is the second death. And whosoever was not found written in the book of life, was cast into the lake of fire."

It is the opinion of some millennarians, and of many who are not, that after the thousand years of peace and purity on earth, there will be a great falling away through the influence of Satan, who will be permitted to go out and seduce the nations to sin; and that so great will be his success, that the number of the seduced will be as the sand of the sea.

This sentiment is derived from the following passage:

"And when the thousand years are expired, Satan shall be loosed out of his prison, and shall go out to deceive the nations, which are in the four quarters of the earth, Gog and Magog, to gather them together to battle: the number of whom is as the sand of the sea. And they went up on the breadth of the earth, and compassed the camp of the saints about, and the beloved city, and fire came down out of heaven and consumed them." It is supposed that this will be permitted, to show that in the devils, the thirst of evil remains unquenched, "and that men, though in conditions most prosperous to their obedience, will, when left by the Spirit, and assailed by temptations, instantly, as in earlier ages revolt, and thus renew the demonstration that their salvation who are redeemed, is wholly of God."

But there is another view of this subject entertained by some, which we will give, and leave the reader to judge which is probably correct.

Who are the nations in the four quarters of the earth whom Satan shall go out to deceive? It is replied, they are the unholy dead, who are raised up simultaneously with the loosing of Satan, in all parts of the world just where they went down to the grave. Included in these vast nations, the number of whom will be as the sands of the sea, will be all the wicked who died before the flood, and who were swept away by that catastrophe, the inhabitants of Sodom and Gomorrah—of Tyre and Sidon, and all the vast nations of antiquity, who were destroyed from earth for their sins. Here, too, will appear the apostate nations, and Gog and Magog, described by Ezekiel, who were destroyed at the commencement of the millennium. Wherever their spirits now are, when the resurrection of their dead bodies shall take place, they will come up just where they died all over and in the four quarters of the world. And they will be just as wicked when they are raised up, and probably more so, as when they passed away from earth, and just as liable to be deceived; for wicked men and seducers shall wax worse and worse, deceiving and being deceived.

These nations, now in the four quarters of the earth, Satan will go out to deceive, under the delusion that, by their aid, he can regain the dominion of the world, and again become its god, the prince of the power of the air, the spirit that now worketh in the children of disobedience. And with this design, it is supposed not to be unnatural that he should aim to deceive, and form into a league with himself, those wicked ones loosed from prison at the same time with himself, and in their resurrection state, now in the four quarters of the earth.

According to this view, it was not the design of God that Satan should be loosed in order that he might tempt, seduce, and deceive the redeemed and sanctified nations; but that he, and all his angels, and all the unholy dead raised up, might come forth to judgment, and that death and the grave might be forever destroyed. Accordingly we find them immediately summoned to judgment.—Rev. 20: 10–15.

This view of the subject, it is thought, is rendered probably correct, from various considerations.

1. According to the account given, the wicked dead are raised at the close of the thousand years simultaneously with the loosing of Satan.

2. There is nothing said of any falling away or apostacy among the redeemed nations.

3. It would seem hardly probable that the King of kings would, having subdued all things to himself, resign his sovereign control, and suffer Satan, a conquered foe, to reusurp the empire of the nations.

4. That there should be such an apostacy, is contrary to prophecy, which declares that when the kingdoms of this world have become the kingdoms of our Lord, he shall rule over them forever, even forever and ever. And Daniel says, that the kingdom which the God of heaven shall set up shall never be destroyed, but shall stand forever. Now, if such a fearful and general apostacy as is supposed should occur, would it not contradict these and many other prophecies equally explicit?

5. This view of the subject does not contradict any other part of scripture, and is in harmony with the purity and blessedness which we may suppose will exist in the new heavens and the new earth, after the restoration of a lost world is fully established.

6. The beloved city and the camp of the saints against which they go up to compass about, are, it is judged, the new Jerusalem, the symbol of the raised and glorified saints, who now, under Christ, have the government of the world. This new Jerusalem—this camp of the saints, is not proba-

bly on earth, but somewhere in mid heavens. If this is correct, then, it would be inappropriate for men in the flesh to come against them, and impossible. But for Satan, and the unholy dead in their resurrection state, to go up against these glorified saints, would be possible; and as the design of the devil is to wrest from them the empire of the world, and defeat their benevolent and holy administration, they are the ones against whom it might reasonably be supposed they would go up. But it will be a deluded, frantic effort, for by the immediately interposing power of God they will be judged every one according to his works, and cast into that place of punishment symbolized by the lake of fire. And this last wicked and Satanic effort to defeat the good, will show the necessity of their doom and vindicate the justice of God in their condemnation.

7. As this view of the subject does not increase the number of the wicked, it accords with all the benevolent promptings of our natures. It would be melancholy to think that after the world had been rescued from the grasp and power of Satan and sin, it should, in a measure, be retaken, and such vast millions perish. All this is obviated by this exposition. Not one more perishes by the loosing of Satan or the resurrection of the unholy dead.

But whatever view of this subject may be adopted as most scriptural and consistent, a difference in opinion here cannot affect the great and fundamental principles and doctrines of the millennarian creed.

How long a time will be occupied in this last scene of judgment is not known; but the great Judge will, no doubt, take time enough to accomplish all his designs, and to make the most impressive moral effect upon the universe. He could, doubtless, in all his acts of judgment, pronounce an unerring decision, and execute his pleasure in an exceedingly short time; but as public judgment is not designed for God himself, but that a finite aud dependent universe may see and understand the rectitude of all his ways, he may, as in many other things, cause the judgment to proceed in orderly progression and development, until every mouth shall be stopped, and all holy beings intelligently respond Amen to all his judgments.

When the judgment is ended, all whose names are not found written in the book of life will be cast into the lake of fire, which is everywhere exhibited as the symbol of the place to which fallen angels and impenitent men will be everlastingly consigned, where they will suffer, not, as we believe, the torment of literal fire; but where, away from God, and the holy, and heaven, they will reap the fruit of their doings—the miseries which sin unpardoned, and an unsanctified and malicious nature, will produce. "The casting of death and hell into the lake of fire denotes that no place of the dead is any more to exist on earth." And thence, onward, the earth will roll on in its endless and glorious career, under the rule of the great King and Mediator between God and man; and the generations of men as they come into the world and fulfill their allotted time and work, will be translated to the glorified without tasting death, as the race of man would have been had sin never entered our world, and had the curse of death never been incurred.

"The last enemy that shall be destroyed is death. And when all things shall be subdued unto him, then shall the Son also be subject unto him that put all things under him, that God may be all in all."—1 Cor. 15: 26-28.

It has been supposed by many, that what the apostle says in this chapter respecting the delivering up of the kingdom to God, even the Father, after all things are subdued under him, has reference to the mediatorial kingdom of Christ, and that consequently from this time onward he will cease to be a mediator. But is it so revealed here, or ever intimated in any other scripture, that Jesus will ever cease to be the mediator between God and man? That Jesus Christ will ever cease to be the mediator, must be seen to be a mere assumption, which cannot be proved. His delivering up the kingdom may mean nothing more than a public and formal announcement that the great work of subduing all enemies, and restoring a lost world, for which all power in heaven and in earth was given unto his hands, is finished—perfectly and forever accomplished. And as that peculiar government over all things, formally given to him for the subjugation of all things, is no longer necessary now that the work is done, it will revert back to the source from which it originated. There is a mystery about this passage which will not probably be removed until the light of another world dawns upon us. But one thing may certainly be affirmed here, that it is not revealed that our Lord will ever lay aside his mediatorial office and character.

When the Son of God so loved our world as voluntarily to assume our nature, it was undoubtedly an eternal union into which he entered with man. He died in our nature, he arose from the tomb in our nature, he ascended on high with our nature, and at the right hand of God, amid the adoring hosts of heaven, he appears in a human form, as the Son of man—the great and glorious mediator.

Now, it is never once intimated that he took upon him our nature for a limited period only, with the design of then casting it off forever as unworthy of him, and worthless; but the whole tenor of revelation is adapted to leave the impression that he formed an eternal union with our nature, and that as our vile bodies at the resurrection are to be changed, and fashioned like unto his glorious body, and a union consummated between him and believers, analagous to a marriage relation, he will be forever presented to them, and associated with them, in his human form, as their great and loved mediator. It must of course be in a modified sense, that he will be the mediator after the last enemy death is destroyed. He will be called upon no longer to exercise his office in the subjugation of sin and the devil; but may he not be, as now, the glorious medium between God and man, through whom all blessings will descend, and all services be rendered?

Viewing the subject in this light, how wonderfully and beyond all comprehension does it magnify the love of Jesus to our world. To be willing to enter into an eternal union with our finite nature, and in the view of principalities and powers to be identified with our race forever, exhibits an affection into which angels may well desire to look. Now, as Christ is to retain our nature forever, he will be a mediator forever, and through him as their Redeemer, the ransomed and holy nations, who shall flourish through eternal ages, will hold communion with the Father of spirits, and render their adoring homage to the Most High.

In conclusion, permit a brief review of the millennarian scheme as here presented, that it may be seen and estimated in a single point of view.

The great and grand idea of millennarianism is the salvation of the world—the complete and eternal restoration of all things to that perfection of holiness and happiness and immortal glory which the scriptures give us to understand would have prevailed had sin never entered. And could any vision of glory and felicity for our miserable world be conceived more beautiful and sublime than this? All else revealed respecting the kingdom of God on earth is subordinate to this grand result, or are only the agencies and means by which it is to be accomplished. For this the new dispensation is to be introduced with means and accompaniments most wisely and effectually adapted to the end designed.

To accomplish this great work, and to perfect it in righteousness, the Lord Jesus Christ will come a second time to our world, at the ushering in of the new economy, without sin, or a sin-offering, unto salvation, to take to himself the sole dominion of the world, and to reign over it forever. To aid in this great work of redeeming love, the saints will be raised and glorified, and as a reward of mercy will be associated with their Lord as his kings and priests, in the government of the unglorified upon earth. To hasten the work, and to cut it short in righteousness, Satan and his hosts will be banished from earth, and ungodly nations and individuals who will not that the Saviour should reign over them, will be judged and destroyed from the earth, as they have been in times past. To renew and sanctify the heart the Spirit will be poured out as showers that water the earth. To cleanse the earth from all pestilential vapors and influences, and to produce a new heavens and a new earth, in which redeemed and restored men may dwell, the fires of the last conflagration will be commissioned to do their work of judgment and regeneration. To administer to the grand result, and to give unity to the race, and harmony to the system, the Jews will be restored ; and Jerusalem, rebuilt, will become the place of divine manifestations, the seat of the Theocracy, whence shall go forth laws and influences which shall preserve the generations of men in uninterrupted harmony, while the Redeemer shall multiply his seed as long as the sun and the moon endure.

Now, what is there low or groveling, earthly, sensual or devilish, in such views as these ? It is a scheme which gives peculiar glory to God, and an infinite expansion to the great designs of his love in human salvation. Is not the restoration of the world, in the sense described, worthy of the Son of God, and worthy of all the agents and instrumentalities to be introduced ? How can it be reconciled with infinite love and wisdom to suppose that sin will be suffered to exist here to the end of time, and that, at last, the earth will be burned up as an accursed thing, and annihilated from being? Would this seem like a triumph on the part of the great Redeemer? Would it not appear that the salvation of Jesus was not equal to the ruin wrought by Satan and sin? But how different the aspect, and infinitely more grand and glorious the whole scheme of Divine love and mercy, when viewed in the light of the millennarian expectation? Oh, what a triumph over Satan and sin, and the curse it will be, when this world is restored to its proper place, amid all the happy orbs which circle the throne of God; and when freed from sin, disease and death, the seed of Christ shall multiply through eternal ages, and thence rise, by transfiguration, to higher scenes in the unfoldings of heaven's glory!

We receive these views, because they seem to us clearly taught in the scriptures of truth. Ridicule, and misrepresent them, ye who will, our souls shall feast on these visions of future glory, while, at the present time, we are called to contend against Satan and sin in patient waiting for the kingdom of God.

The complete salvation or restoration of our world being the great end to be attained, it may easily be seen that the agencies and means revealed are fully adequate and wisely adapted to its accomplishment.

1. To convert the world, there needs to be produced a certain and indubitable conviction of the truth. One of the most formidable obstacles in the way of the salvation of men at present, is the unbelief which prevails in unnumbered forms and degrees around the world, and the errors and diversities of doctrines which exist among those who profess the truth. Something must be done to expel this skepticism, and to drive away these fogs of error and delusion, which have settled so densely around the minds of so many.

Now, how gloriously adapted to this end will be the personal appearing of the Son of Man! Oh, what.convictions, certain and indubitable, would this produce! And now, if our Lord should thus condescend to come, who dare say it would not be a blessing, and would not, beyond conception, subserve the cause of truth and righteousness? His appearing in personal glory would undoubtedly be just as wisely adapted to convince men of the truth, as was his appearing to Saul of Tarsus.

2. To effect a complete restoration of mankind to holiness and happiness, it seems necessary that Satanic influence, and those fearful temptations to sin which now are seen to exist, should be removed from the world. So the scriptures teach, that before the salvation of the world is attained, Satan shall be bound and cast into the pit, and that all the tares, the children of the wicked one, who are too deeply depraved to be reformed, shall be gathered out of the world by the command of the Lord. Thus will the strong man be bound and his goods spoiled.

3. Spiritual influences and agencies, such as have never yet been enjoyed will be necessary to convert our fallen world to an abode of righteousness. Accordingly we find it predicted in various scriptures that in the last days there shall be the most abundant and remarkable outpourings of the Spirit of God upon all flesh, who together shall see his salvation. And then in connection with all this there will be the ministration of the saints raised and glorified, frequently appearing and holding intercourse with the living, and guiding them by their instructions and influence, to holy and happy pursuits.

And then these things will take place, too, in a physically regenerated earth, where means for the restoration of man's physical nature, in harmony with his spritual, will be provided, in the leaves of the tree of life, which are for the healing of the nations.

Thus, it is manifest that the agencies and means revealed in scripture, are fully adequate to the end proposed, and wisely adapted.

And then let it be borne in mind, that all these will be added to all divinely appointed human instrumentalities on earth. The converted Jews and Gentiles will joyfully and harmoniously be workers together with God, in working out their own and other's salvation, and hence all the powers of heaven and earth will conspire to one and the same sublime result.

It is altogether an unauthorized assumption, that God intends to convert the world simply and solely through those agencies which are now employed. God intends, by present means, in connection with the publishing of the gospel to all nations, to gather out of them a people for his name, and to prepare the way for the introduction of a new and brighter era. And hence, it is a great and momentous work in which we are engaged, in which we have the most abundant encouragement to labor and pray, in the hope that we may save many from sin, and prepare the way for the kingdom of heaven.

It is often said of millennarian views, that they have no practical tendency, but discourage effort, and hence are only evil in their tendency and influence.

These views teach us to associate the hopes of our world with the second glorious appearing of Christ, and it is by his appearing, or by considerations thence derived, that we are exhorted in scripture to every good word and work, to do his will.

To show the practical tendency of the second advent, and the consequent importance of this truth, as a motive to all that is good, attention is directed to the following scriptures :

By considerations drawn from the coming, the appearing, or revelation of Jesus Christ, we are exhorted—

1. To repentance.

"Repent ye, therefore, and be converted, that your sins may be blotted out, when the times of refreshing shall come from the presence of the Lord, *and he shall send Jesus Christ,* whom the heavens must receive until the times of the restitution of all things," &c.—Acts. 3 : 19, 20.

2. To love Christ.

"If any man love not the Lord Jesus Christ, let him be Anathema Maranatha"—which, being interpreted, is, Let him be accursed when the Lord cometh.

3. To love one another.

"And the Lord make you to increase and abound in love towards one another, and towards all men, even as we do toward you: to the end he may establish your hearts unblameable in holiness before God, even our Father, *at the coming of our Lord Jesus Christ with all his saints.*"—1 Thess. 3 : 13.

4. To mortification of worldly lusts.

"When Christ, who is our life, *shall appear, then* shall ye also appear with him in glory. Mortify, *therefore,* your members which are upon earth; fornication, uncleanness, inordinate affection, evil concupisence, and covetousness, which is idolatry."—Col. 3 : 4, 5.

"The grace of God that bringeth salvation hath appeared to all men, teaching us, that denying ungodliness and worldly lusts, we should live soberly, righteously, and godly, in this present world; looking for that blessed hope, *even the glorious appearing* of the great God, our Saviour Jesus Christ." Titus 2 : 11–13.

5. To general obedience and holiness.

"For the Son of man shall come in the glory of his Father with his angels; and then shall he reward every man according to his works.

"And now, little children, abide in him, that *when he shall appear*, we may have confidence, and not be ashamed before him *at his coming*.

"We know that when he shall appear, we shall be like him; for we shall see him as he is. And every man that hath this hope in him purifieth himself even as he is pure." —1 John 2: 8, and 3: 2, 3.

6. To spirituality of mind.

"For our conversation is in heaven; *from whence also we look for the Saviour*, the Lord Jesus Christ; who shall change our vile bodies," &c.—Phil 3: 20, 21.

7. To watchfulness.

"Watch, therefore; for ye know not what hour your Lord will come. Therefore be ye also ready; for, in such an hour as ye think not, the Son of man cometh."—Math. 24: 42–44.

"But ye, brethren, are not in darkness, that that day should overtake you as a thief: ye are all the children of light, and of the day; therefore let us not sleep as do others; but let us watch and be sober."—1 Thess. 5: 4–6.

8. To patience and long-suffering.

"For ye have need of patience, that after ye have done the will of God, ye might receive the promise: for yet a little while, and he that shall come will come and will not tarry." —Heb. 10: 36, 37.

"Be patient therefore, brethren, unto *the coming of the Lord*."—James 5: 7, 8.

"That the trial of your faith, being much more precious than of gold that perisheth, though it be tried with fire, might be found unto praise, and honor, and glory *at the appearing of Jesus Christ*."—1 Peter 1: 6, 7.

"Beloved, think it not strange concerning the fiery trial which is to try you, as though some strange thing happened unto you; but rejoice, inasmuch as ye are partakers of

Christ's sufferings; *that when his glory is revealed* ye may be glad also with exceeding joy."—1 Pet. 4: 12, 13.

9. To ministerial fidelity.

Who is a faithful and wise servant, whom his lord hath made ruler over his household, to give them meat in due season? Blessed is that servant whom his lord, *when he cometh,* shall find so doing.—Matt. 24: 46.

"I give thee charge, in the sight of God, who quickeneth all things; and before Jesus Christ, who, before Pontius Pilate, witnessed a good confession; that thou keep this commandment without spot, unrebukable, *until the appearing of our Lord Jesus Christ.*"—1 Tim. 6: 13, 14.

"I charge thee before God and the Lord Jesus Christ, who shall judge the quick and the dead *at his appearing and kingdom,* preach the word," &c.—2 Tim. 4: 1, 2.

These scriptures might be greatly multiplied in which we are referred directly to the second coming of our Lord, and the appearing at that time of his glorious kingdom, for the most solemn and weighty motives to obedience, and to the cultivation and practice of all that is good. How, then, can any truthfully say that there is no practical tendency in millennarian views, which, in entire harmony with these scriptures, direct us continually to the coming of our Lord, as our blessed hope, for motive to every good word and work? Surely we cannot err far from the right way while we follow the teachings of our Lord and his apostles, and warn, and exhort, and entreat, and persuade men by the coming of our Lord Jesus Christ, with all his saints, to live soberly and righteously in the present world, and to cherish all the graces, and do all the works which he has enjoined.

Now, it is a remarkable fact, that while there are so many scriptures directing us to the second coming of Christ, and exhorting us to live and act in reference to it, there is not one which exhorts or commands us to expect, or to labor for the conversion of the world before he comes. If there is, let it be produced, and we will confess our error.

The fact is, nothing could be more eminently practical than the millennarian expectation—nothing better adapted to lessen our love for the present world—to humble us before God, and to lead us, in the hope of his appearing, to purify ourselves even as he is pure.

"Blessed is that servant whom his Lord, when he cometh, shall find so doing. Amen. Come, Lord Jesus, come quickly."

Chapter Eighth.

THE SEASON AND SIGNS OF CHRIST'S COMING.

But when shall these things be, and what shall be the sign of his coming, and of the end of the dispensation?

These have been the mysteries into which curiosity in every age has inquired most diligently, and in respect to which presumption has most widely and extravagantly erred. During the life of our Saviour, the time when he was to come, and when his kingdom was to appear, were subjects of deepest interest to friends and foes. But to all such inquiries our Lord gave but one general answer: "Of that day and hour knoweth no man." "It is not given to you to know the times and the seasons which the Father hath placed in his own power." And in accordance with these assurances that none can know definitely beforehand when the Son of Man will come, and when his kingdom will appear, our Lord uniformly exhorted, "Be ye also ready, for in such an hour as ye think not the Son of Man will come." "And take heed to yourselves, lest at any time your hearts be overcharged with surfeiting, and drunkenness, and cares of this life, and so that day come upon you unawares. For as a snare shall it come on all them that dwell on the face of the whole earth. Watch ye, therefore, and pray always, that ye may be accounted worthy to escape all these things that shall come to pass, and to stand before the Son of Man."

It is clearly the design of God that "That day should be unknown to men, that they may shake off all carnal security, and be always watchful, because they know not at what hour the Lord will come; and may be ever prepared to say, 'Come, Lord Jesus, come quickly. Amen.'"—*Confession of Faith.*

Now, just here has been the fatal rock upon which many have made shipwreck, in attempting to fix that which God in revelation has not fixed, and to reveal what the Father has seen best to reserve to himself. History shows that the great error and prolific evil on this subject has not been in "looking for that blessed hope, even the glorious appearing of the great God our Saviour," but in fixing the day or the hour, which no man can know. And is it any wonder that when men attempt to be wise above that which is written, that God should leave them to wide mistake, delusion, and shame?

But though our Lord has definitely taught that the time of his advent and the appearing of his kingdom will not be known to men until it bursts in literal splendor on the world, yet, to gratify a reasonable curiosity, and to sustain and strengthen the faith of his people, and exalt their hopes, he has in prophecy laid down certain infallible signs which are to indicate the near approach of his glorious appearing and kingdom.

And there is no contradiction between the statement that, of that day and hour knoweth no man, and the fact that our Lord has given certain great predicted signs and chronological epochs which are to foreshadow his approach. It would be perfectly proper to say of any man, that of the day and the hour of his death, none know; but that his declining old age, his faltering steps and failing powers, would indicate the rapid advance of dissolution. So, also, the fact that our Lord and his apostles and prophets have foretold some of the great events which are to come to pass before his advent, and which are to indicate its near aproach, does not conflict with the truth, that of the day and hour of his coming knoweth no man. Some of the events which are immediately to precede and foreshadow our Lord's coming are of a most fearful and afflictive character; and had they not been announced in prophecy, so that their relation to the coming kingdom might be known, they might have overwhelmed the people of God in hopeless despair; but as they are announced as indicating his coming, they furnish the strongest ground for faith and hope.

As it is not designed to go into any particular exposition of the symbolical prophecies of the Revelations, we shall confine our remarks to some of the more obvious teachings of our Lord and his apostles.

1. One prominent premonitory sign which will indicate the near approach of the end of the present dispensation, and the coming of our Lord, will be the preaching of the gospel unto all nations as a witness. Matt. 24: 14. "And this gospel of the kingdom shall be preached into all the world, for a witness unto all nations; and then shall the end come."

What end is here meant? Not certainly the end—the ταλος—the consummation of the Jewish dispensation; for that certainly was consummated at the crucifixion of our Lord, when on the cross, he cried out, "It is finished," and died. And this was before the gospel was preached to the Gentile nations, and into all the world. Hence, it is certain that the termination of the Jewish dispensation is not intended here.

Nor can it mean, we judge, the destruction of Jerusalem, and the dispersion of the Jews into all nations; for what relation could the preaching of the gospel of the kingdom into all the world as a witness have to the destruction of Jerusalem, and the dispersion of the Israelitish nation? And, besides, it has never yet been proved that the gospel was preached literally unto all the world, before the breaking up of the nation of the Jews; and if it was not, then the declaration of our Lord that the end would immediately, or soon come after the publication of the gospel of the kingdom into all the world as a witness, must refer to some future event.

This declaration of our Lord is, we judge, identical with the prophecy of Daniel, that as the time of the end draws near, "Many shall run to and fro, and knowledge shall be increased."

Daniel 12: 4. "But thou, O Daniel, shut up the words, and seal the book, even to the time of the end: Many shall run to and fro, and knowledge shall be increased."

Take whatever view we may of the import of this passage, none can fail to see how literally it is being fulfilled at the present, in connection with the efforts in every Christian land to publish the gospel as speedily as possible unto all nations. Never, since the creation of the world, was there an age like the present, when knowledge upon every subject was so rapidly and universally diffused. The world seems to be in a whirl, as if in preparation for some great event. Many are literally running to and fro on railroads, and steamships, and magnetic telegraphs, and through the activities of the press, as if the time was short, and in anticipation of some undefined grand developments in the future.

Or, if we confine the prophecy within narrower limits, and restrict it to the increase of gospel knowledge, its fulfillment is no less remarkable. How wonderfully has the Christian world waked up in these last days to their obligations to the heathen, and how, in obedience to the dictates of the love and command of Jesus, are many hastening into every accessible nation, and into every island of the sea, to teach and to publish to them the glad tidings of a Saviour's love! The preachers and missionaries of the gospel are even now running to and fro, from north to south, and east to west, into almost every part of the habitable world. How remarkably and wonderfully do all the activities of the present day accord with the scriptures of truth, and harmonize with millennarian expectation! "Verily, we have in these things a spirit-stirring and portentous sign of the coming of the kingdom of God, when, if the nations will not embrace the gospel, and submit to his sway, He shall break them with a rod of iron, and dash them in pieces as a potter's vessel."

As the time of the end draws on, this last fact will probably be associated with the publishing of the gospel to all nations, as a fearful and portentous reality, as indicated in Revelations 14: 6:—

"And I saw another angel fly in the midst of heaven, having the everlasting gospel to preach unto them that dwell on the earth, and to every nation, and kindred, and tongue, and people, saying with a loud voice, Fear God, and give glory to him; for the hour of his judgment is come." Already this is being extensively done, and not only millennarians, but many who are not, are predicting that some fearful and desolating revolutions will soon sweep over the despotic and apostate nations of Europe especially, and perhaps embrace in their outer circles other and distant nations.

The preaching of the gospel of the kingdom, then, in these last times, into all the habitable world, and the rapid and vast increase of gospel and other knowledge, as predicted to precede and foreshadow the end of the present dispensation and the coming of the Son of Man, furnish conclusive indication that we are drawing nigh to the great crisis in human affairs, and the realization of the world's glorious hope.

2. Another premonitory symptom which will indicate the near approach of the Son of Man, will be the increase and wide-spread of skepticism in regard to the truth of God in general, and in respect to the second coming of our Lord in particular.

The apostle Paul says, "Now the Spirit speaketh expressly, that in the latter times, some shall depart from the faith, giving heed to seducing spirits, and doctrines of devils." —1 Tim. 4: 1.

"But, beloved, remember ye the words which were spoken before, of the apostles of our Lord Jesus Christ; How that they told you there should be mockers in the last times, who shall walk after their own lusts."—Jude 17: 18.

"For the time will come, when they will not endure sound doctrines; but after their own lusts shall they heap to themselves teachers having itching ears; and they shall turn away their ears from the truth, and shall be turned unto fables."—2 Tim. 4: 3, 4.

These scriptures, in connection with many others, indicate the wide and rapid spread of infidelity in various forms, in the last times of the present dispensation. And, now, what are the facts in the case? Never, since the times of the apostles, has infidelity been so painfully and alarmingly prevalent as at the present day. It is not our intention to attempt to trace the causes of this, or to give statistics on the subject. The fact is very generally acknowledged and felt. Infidels themselves boast, and truthfully too, of their own rapid increase, and most who are conversant with the world are forced, from painful observation, to believe. Everything seems to be made tributary to its increase. A perverted view of the sciences, phrenology, mesmerism, spiritual rappings, in connection with the divided state of the Christian church, all are made subservient to the denial of the truth. Tributary also to this vast stream of unbelief which is spreading over the world, are the prolific issues of the press, of a light, corrupt, and demoralizing literature, which is more eagerly sought and read by the great masses, than any other. And this infidelity is not only seen outside of the church, but within its bosom is witnessed, in many cases, its undermining process.

The prospects would be exceedingly discouraging, and we should almost yield ourselves to utter despondency, did we not know that the Lord reigns, and were we not assured that this increase and wide spread of infidelity, is one of the signs which is to precede the ushering in of a brighter day, when truth beaming from the personal presence of the Sun of righteousness, shall dispel error and delusion from the world.

Let skeptics then be warned, that that same word which predicts their rise and spread, foretells their overthrow and ruin at the last. Let them not, then, rejoice too loudly or boast too confidently, for they are only a sign of a coming God, and a solemn retribution.

But this infidelity without and within the church, is to be especially manifested in opposition to the second literal and personal coming of our Lord. Peter says, "Knowing this first, that there shall come, in the last days, scoffers, walking after their own lusts, and saying, Where is the promise of his coming? for since the fathers fell asleep, all things continue as they were from the beginning of the creation."—2 Peter 3: 3, 4.

Let it be noticed that this is to be one of the characteristics of the last days. And is it not true of the present time? Infidels universally deny the coming of our Lord, and often employ the very argument here predicted, drawn from the stability of nature's laws, to refute the Christian.

From the fact that the second coming of Christ is becoming a prominent theme in the church, infidelity is found to be arrayed against this article of faith in particular.

And then, in addition to all this, there are various sects, one of whose prominent article is, a denial of the second literal coming of Christ. Swedenborgians deny this as one of their fundamental principles. Universalists deny the coming of our Lord to judgment, and so of other sects equally important. And then, too, in many evangelical churches, it is a subject seldom dwelt upon, as having any practical importance in the publication of the gospel. These things are certainly portentous, and show that we are verily living in the last days. And the more the enemy triumphs, and the more generally the coming of our Lord is denied and ridiculed, the more ardently and confidently shall we look for his glorious appearing soon to take place.

Painful, then, as are the developments of infidelity, delusion, and error, Christians should not be disheartened or discouraged, knowing that in proportion as scoffers arise in the last times, the day of redemption draweth nigh. Let us watch and pray, that we enter not into temptation, and are not seduced from the simplicity of the truth as it is in Jesus, by the devices of the wicked one.

3. The time of our Lord's coming, he assures us, will be indicated by violent political agitations and revolutions, and a season of unwonted distress and perplexity among the nations.

In the twenty-first chapter of Luke, having described the destruction of Jerusalem, and the dispersion of the Jews into all nations, in the twenty-fifth verse and onward, he foretells the signs which are to precede and denote the near approach of his second advent.

"And there shall be signs in the sun, and in the moon, and in the stars; and upon the earth distress of nations, with perplexity; the sea and the waves roaring; men's hearts failing them for fear, and for looking after those things which are coming on the earth: for the powers of heaven shall be shaken. And then shall they see the Son of Man coming in a cloud, with power and great glory. And when these things begin to come to pass, then look up, and lift up your heads: for your redemption draweth nigh."

The signs in the sun, moon, and stars, and earth, do not denote mere phenomena of the material world; but are manifestly employed as symbols of great political revolutions, and popular tumults, and disastrous commotions, on earth. The sun, moon, and stars, represent monarchs, princes, nobles and subordinate rulers, who exert a power and influence over men, analagous to that which the heavenly bodies exert upon the material world; while the sea and the waves roaring represent the people in insurrection, and commotion, and tumult. Understanding the symbols in these senses, no language could more forcibly describe a series of fearful and violent political convulsions and revolutions, by which monarchs and princes, and officers of state, these powers of heaven shall be shaken, and their thrones be tossed and dashed by popular violence, as vessels upon the bosom of raging billows. It is easy to conceive that amid such disastrous commotions, there may be upon the earth great distress of nations with perplexity. Men will not know what to do, or what course to take, and their hearts will fail them for fear, and for looking after those things which are coming upon the earth. Now, when such a state of things shall come to pass on the earth, then we are assured that the coming of the Son of Man is nigh, even at the door.

And from indications, such a state of things seems to be not far distant from the European nations. As coming events commonly cast their shadows before them, so the shadows of vast political revolutions, and insurrections and blood, have fallen on the minds of most men who are acquainted with passing events. There are, at this time, fearful apprehensions on the minds of very many. Already there is perplexity and a portentous looking after those things which are coming upon the earth. A few years will perhaps develop scenes of revolution and blood such as the world has never before witnessed. Europe has vast arrears to settle with the God of providence. She has shed the blood of the saints, and she shall have blood to drink. These nations have downtrodden and cruelly oppressed the Jews, and God has said that he will make a full end of the nations that have oppressed them. Whoever is looking for peaceful and happy republics in Europe, then, will look in vain. Nought but oppression, revolution and blood, await them until the coming of the Son of Man.

Should the revolutions and wars which are now so generally anticipated, correspond in their perplexing and distressful character to the description of our Lord, then we might confidently look up, and lift up our heads, knowing that the Redeemer of men was nigh his coming.

To show the relation of these things to the time of his advent, he spoke a parable: "And he spake to them a parable; Behold the fig-tree, and all the trees; when they now shoot forth, ye see and know of your own selves that summer is now nigh at hand. So likewise ye, when ye see these things come to pass, know ye that the kingdom of God is nigh at hand. Verily, I say unto you, This generation shall not pass away, till all these things be fulfilled." From this last declaration it has commonly been supposed that our Lord spoke only of the destruction of Jerusalem, and attending events, and that all must have occurred before those then living had all passed away from earth. But there is no necessity for such a construction. The word translated generation, ἡ γενεα, does not uniformly denote the men of a particular time or age, but a posterity of any man, a line of descendants, a race, or class of people, extending in regular descent over indefinite ages. Did time permit, many examples might be given of the use of the word in this sense.

The term, in this sense, then may denote the Jewish race, or descendants. The Saviour meant this race of people, the Jews, should not pass away, or be destroyed, till all was fulfilled. And now, what are the facts in the case? The Jews, as a race or generation, still remain. No powers have been able to crush or annihilate them. They live a miracle of providence, and witnesses to his truth, that all will yet be fulfilled which is predicted.

Their literal preservation as a race furnishes an assurance of the correctness of the exposition given.

Intimately associated with the violent political revolutions and distress of nations, spoken of in the above prediction, and perhaps identified with them, is the time of unprecedented trouble predicted by our Lord, as recorded in Matthew, and by the prophets Daniel and Jeremiah.

Matt. 24: 21, 22. "For there shall be great tribulation, such as was not since the beginning of the world, to this time; no, nor ever shall be. And except those days should be shortened, there should no flesh be saved: but for the elect's sake those days shall be shortened."

It is commonly supposed, that this time of trouble was experienced at the destruction of Jerusalem, and the dispersion of the Jews by the Romans. But there are certain intimations in the passage itself, and in other parallel scriptures, which show that if this was included it was by no means all that was meant. The prophet Daniel says, 12: 1, 2, "And at that time shall Michael stand up, the great prince which standeth for the children of thy people: And there shall be a time of trouble, *such as never was since there was a nation,* even to that same time: and at that time thy people shall be delivered, every one that shall be found written in the book. And many of them that sleep in the dust of the earth shall awake, some to everlasting life, and some to shame and everlasting contempt."

Jeremiah says, "Alas! for that day is great, *so that none is like it*; it is even the time of Jacob's trouble, but he shall be saved out of it. For it shall come to pass in that day, saith the Lord of hosts, that I will break his yoke from off thy neck, and will burst thy bonds, and strangers shall no more serve themselves of him: But they shall serve the Lord their God, and David, their king, whom I will raise up unto them."

Now, here are three different sacred writers who predict a time of trouble in respect to the Jews especially, of which it is said: There shall be none like it—such as never was since there was a nation, or from the creation, or ever shall be. But there can be only one such time of trouble, of which it can be truly said, there is none like it, or that it is greater than all others. Hence it is certain that our Lord, Daniel, and Jeremiah, must refer to the same time or season of trouble; for it would be charging our Lord, or the prophets with untruth in their representations, to assume that they referred to different times, when each declares of the time of which he speaks that there is, or will be, none like it.

Regarding this, therefore, as a settled point, that but one time of unprecedented trouble is referred to in these separate predictions, there are some marks here which show that neither our Lord nor the prophets referred to the destruction of Jerusalem.

1. Both Daniel and Jeremiah associate their time of trouble with the salvation of the Jews. "At that time," says Daniel, "shall thy people be delivered;" and Jeremiah says, "but Jacob shall be saved out of it." Now, these could not refer to the trouble experienced at the destruction of Jerusalem, for the people were not then delivered or saved, neither did they then serve the Lord their God, and David, their king, or Christ, as predicted, as an immediate consequence and result of this time of trouble, according to Jeremiah.

2. The time of trouble of which Daniel speaks, and of which he says, there was never any like it, is associated with a resurrection of the dead. "And many of them which sleep in the dust of the earth shall awake." As there was no resurrection at the time of Jerusalem's destruction, and the dispersion of the nation, it is clear that the prophet must have had his eye on some event long after this, which is to occur immediately preceding a resurrection. But as our Lord says, of his time of trouble, that there shall never be any so great afterward; and as the prophet declares of his, that it shall be so terrible, that never before was there anything like it, it is rendered certain that they must both refer to the same terrible scene, and that it must be in the last times, immediately preceding a resurrection of some of the dead, and the deliverance of the Jews from their unbelief and dispersion.

3. These conclusions are confirmed by what our Lord says of his: "And except those days should be shortened, there should no flesh be saved; but for the elect's sake those days shall be shortened."

Now, the days of Israel's troubles were not shortened, but the destruction of their city, and the dispersion of the nation, were only the beginnings of sorrow, which have been perpetuated through eighteen centuries. Let any one carefully examine their history, and he will see that they have suffered repeatedly as great and accumulated sorrows as at the first. Now, as their time of trouble was not shortened, and as our Lord declares, in regard to the time of trouble of which he speaks, that it shall be shortened, it follows that it was not really to the troubles attending the destruction of Jerusalem that he referred, but to that represented by Jeremiah and Daniel, when Israel shall be delivered and saved.

4. And then the troubles attending the destruction of Jerusalem by the Romans, was limited to one nation, but the

time of trouble of which our Lord speaks, is to be so wide, circling, and comprehensive of all nations, that unless these days of sorrow were shortened, *no flesh* should be saved. This shows that a time of trouble, far more terrible, wide-wasting and desolating, than has ever been experienced, is meant—a time of trouble so dreadful, that unless the Lord interposes, and cuts short the days, one universal ruin would sweep over the world.

There is, then, according to prophecy, a day of fearful trial and tribulation, and darkness, yet to come upon the world, before that brighter day, when the Lord shall reign on Mount Zion, and execute righteousness and judgment in the earth. Men may cry, peace, peace; but God hath said, there is no peace to the wicked, and he has never said there shall be peace until the Lord comes.

And with these things agree all the prophets. Joel says, "Blow ye the trumpet in Zion, and sound an alarm in my holy mountain; let all the inhabitants of the land tremble: for the day of the Lord cometh, for it is nigh at hand: A day of darkness and of gloominess, a day of clouds and of thick darkness, as the morning spread upon the mountains: a great people and strong; *there hath not been ever the like, neither shall be any more after it,* even to the years of many generations. A fire devoureth before them; and behind them a flame burneth; the land is as the garden of Eden before them, and behind them a desolate wilderness; yea, and nothing shall escape them. Before their face the people shall be much pained: all faces shall gather blackness. The earth shall quake before them; the heavens shall tremble: the sun and the moon shall be dark, and the stars shall withdraw their shining: And the Lord shall utter his voice before his army: for his camp is very great: for he is strong that executeth his word: for the day of the Lord is great and very terrible; and who can abide it?"—Joel 2: 1–3, 6: 10–12.

It is manifest, that the prophet Joel here refers to, and describes the same time of trouble and destruction, as did Jeremiah, Daniel, and our Lord; for he gives the same unprecedented characteristic respecting it, "There hath not been ever the like, neither shall be any more after it." And he also associates it with the deliverance and salvation of Israel, especially, as any one may see by reading the chapter.

And, according to the clear intimations of prophecy, it would not be surprising if we should see the beginnings of this sorrow in our own days, or if not, that they should occur in the days of our children. And how strikingly does all this harmonize with the annunciation of the angel of the Apocalypse, commissioned to preach the everlasting gospel to the nations!

"And I saw another angel fly in the midst of heaven, having the everlasting gospel to preach unto them that dwell on the earth, and to every nation, and kindred, and tongue, and people, saying, with a loud voice, Fear God, and give glory to him: *for the hour of* his judgment *is come:* and worship him that made heaven, and earth, and the sea, and the fountains of waters."—Rev. 14: 6, 7.

Now, should such a time of trouble come upon the world as is here predicted, the faithful should not despond, but regard it as an omen of the near approach of a peaceful and glorious day.

4. Intimately associated with this unprecedented time of trouble, and perhaps in connection with it, and a part of it, it is believed by many that the time of our Lord's advent will be preceded by a simultaneous, terrible, and bloody persecution of the true worshippers of God, or the two witnesses spoken of in Revelations 11: 3, 13. The two witnesses are the two

olive trees, and the two lamps representing the teachers or preachers of the true gospel, and the faithful who receive and live according to their teachings. The prescribed limits of this work will not permit a discussion of this subject. All that can now be said is, that there is reason to believe from prophecy, that there will yet be a combination of papal, apostate, and infidel powers, against the true spiritual worshippers of the Lord, and a bloody slaughter. And it would seem as if we were permitted already to hear the rumbling of their distant thunder, and the menaces of their wrath.

But, when these enemies have done their worst, their triumph shall be short, for, "For the Elect's sake, those days shall be shortened," and God the Redeemer will appear for the deliverance and triumph eternally of his people.

We are aware that this is a painful view of things, but what can be gained by closing our ears from the admonitory voice of God, and thus suffer that day to come upon us unawares and unprepared? Let all men, let the nations know that God has written these things in his book, that when they come to pass, they may know that God is true and just. And ye professed disciples of Jesus, "Take heed to yourselves, lest at any time your hearts be overcharged with surfeiting and drunkenness, and cares of this life, and so that day come upon you unawares. For, as a snare shall it come on all them that dwell on the face of the earth."

5. The prophecies give us to understand, that prior to our Lords coming there will be an effort to restore the Jews, and a partial restoration probably take place. Should we see any such movement, we should regard it as a clear scriptural sign of our Lord's near approach.

6. It is believed that, as the time of the end draws nigh, and as iniquity abounds, the love of many in the church will wax cold, and a very general declension in true, self-denying, spiritual religion take place. Our Lord alludes to this, when

he says, in Matthew 24th, "And because iniquity shall abound, the love of many shall wax cold." And the apostle Paul probably looked down to this, as well as to all the apostacies which have occurred under the Christian dispensation, when he said—

"This know also, that in the last days perilous times shall come. For men shall be lovers of their own selves, pre-eminently selfish, covetous, boasters, proud, blasphemers, disobedient to parents, unthankful, unholy, without natural affection, truce-breakers, false accusers, incontinent, fierce, despisers of those that are good, traitors, heady, high-minded, lovers of pleasure more than lovers of God; having a form of godliness, but denying the power thereof."

The vices which are here named are most of them detailed in the first chapter of Romans, as characteristic of the heathen world; but from the fact that he here states that these vices are to prevail among those who have a form of godliness, while they deny the power thereof, it appears that it is a state of things particularly in connection with the church or professors of religion that is described. These vices have always prevailed among men, and do now; but they are to have a peculiar and perilous manifestation under the garb of godliness.

From many considerations which might be dwelt upon, it would really seem that we are rapidly falling upon the times here denoted. The vast revivals of formalism, and the increase of those sects which repudiate the influences of the Spirit, together with the unwonted incentives to worldliness, lust, and pleasure, which exist at the present day, are tending to the very results predicted. Whether the world is really growing better or worse, is a question which does not belong to, or in any way affect the main points of millenarianism, and perhaps it would be difficult for us who live and act in the midst of present scenes to determine. But men are apt to be amazingly deceived by external appearances, and to mistake the progress of mere worldly knowledge and improvement for that vital godliness which sanctifies and prepares for heaven.

There is, no doubt, a vast increase of knowledge, and there are equally great improvements in the arts of civilization, in the facilities of intercourse, and the general supply of human wants. But whither are these things tending? Are men, within and without the church, becoming less selfish, less worldly, less sensual, less in love with things of time and sense, and more and more Godlike, and devoted to the things which pertain to the kingdom of God?

We are to bear in mind that there is no religion in railroads, steamships, magnetic telegraphs, printing-presses, or in the progress of the arts and sciences, in themselves considered. Unsanctified and unappropriated to the glory and service of God, they may all become instruments of unrighteousness, and may afford such powerful stimulus to avarice, to worldliness, to selfishness in every form, and pleasure, that God, and the world to come may be left wholly out of view. And there is ground for serious apprehension that such are, in fact, the practical effects which are being produced.

When we speak of the world growing worse or better, we speak only in respect to religion, pure and undefiled before God—that religion which purifies the heart, and overcomes the world, which rejoices in the truth, and which kindles in the heart hungering and thirsting after righteousness, as the object of supreme desire. Is there such a growing holiness in the church, including all the sects in Christendom? Do the world take knowledge of Christians that they are less covetous, less devoted to the love of the things of time, more upright in their dealings, more conscientious, more punctual and faithful in all their engagements, more self-denying for the cause of Jesus, more solicitous for the glory of God than themselves, and more anxious to secure eternal life for themselves and others, than anything in the form of wealth, or honor, or pleasure, which this world can present? Alas, we fear the reverse is too true.

Undoubtedly, this is an age of benevolent effort, and there are many bright examples of self-sacrifice in the devoted men who have gone forth to publish the gospel to all nations, and also in those at home, who sustain them. But is this the case generally? O, how hard it is, and how many agents and agencies are required to draw out from the churches the little that is necessary to meet the demands of a perishing world.

We maintain that, in no gospel sense, is the world growing better, or the church becoming purer, only in proportion as men love God and keep his commandments, and seek as their great object to lay up treasures in heaven and not on earth. Let any minister sit down candidly, and ask himself, Do I find in my experience that Christians are growing in love for one another, that mutual confidence is increasing, that true spirituality and heavenly-mindedness are acquiring a greater and greater ascendancy, that revivals are consequently more frequent, deep and permanent, and that the love and obedience of Christ are becoming the great and all-controlling principle of action, to an unwonted and delightful extent? Or does it rather require all my efforts to resist, if possible, the downward tendency of things, and to strengthen the things that remain and are ready to die? and we believe there will be but one verdict in respect to the aspect of things.

Now, our hearts would sicken and die, were we not permitted to read in the book of prophecy that in the last days great vices shall prevail under a form of godliness, that perilous times shall come in respect to true piety, and that because iniquity shall abound the love of many shall wax cold; but that just beyond is a brighter day, when the enemies of the truth shall be confounded, and the Sun of righteousness arise with healing in his beams, to scatter forever the darkness of error and sin.

Let skeptics and hostile sects rejoice, then, if they will, over the decline of vital godliness in Christian churches, and say, Aha! So would we have it; we know that as surely as God reigns, these are only one of the signs which are to precede and foreshadow the dawn of a millennial day.

"Behold, I come as a thief. Blessed is he that watcheth, and keepeth his garments, lest he walk naked, and they see his shame. He that overcometh, the same shall be clothed in white raiment; and I will not blot out his name out of the book of life, but I will confess his name before my Father, and before his angels."

7. As another indication which shall mark the near approach of our Lord, He says, "For there shall arise false Christs, and false prophets, or teachers, and shall show great signs and wonders; insomuch, that if it were possible, they shall deceive the very elect. Behold I have told you before. Wherefore, if they shall say unto you, Behold, he is in the desert, go not forth; behold, he is in the secret chambers, believe it not. For as the lightning cometh out of the east, and shineth even unto the west, so also shall the coming of the Son of Man be."

In view of these things, we are not surprised to see such pretenders as the various Mormon prophets, as A. J. Davis, and other professed spiritual mediums arise, and by showing signs and wonders deceive many.

Nor are we surprised to see false teachers of various names and pretensions, rising up thick and numberless around, propagating all kinds of errors, and giving birth to all kinds of absurd opinions.

We expect, as the day of deliverance draws on, these will multiply, and their adherents increase; and many of them will seem so reasonable, and so pleasing, and will show such signs and wonders that they shall deceive, if it were possible, the true people of God. Let all who love the truth, then, beware of false teachers, and let them watch and pray lest they enter into temptations, and be seduced from the faith once delivered to the saints, for it is certain that the devil will yet come down, with many lying wonders, and great wrath, knowing that his time is short.

8. The chronological data which the prophecies give, furnish intimations that the time is short when all that is predicted shall come to pass.

One of the most prominent periods fixed for the termination of the 1260 years so repeatedly brought to view in the prophecies of Daniel and John, is 1866. This clearly does not mark the time of the coming of the Son of Man, for that time none can know; but according to prophecy, within the limits of some four years from that time, preceding or succeeding, may be expected a great crisis in the political affairs of the nations, and great revolutions, which may dissolve the relation between church and state in Europe, and have a most important bearing upon the Jewish people, in preparing the way for their ultimate restoration in part to their own land.

Precisely what course these political events are to take, it would be hazardous to state, for it is not revealed; but there is clear intimation in prophecy that Russia is yet to gain an entire ascendancy over continental Europe, and have all the powers thereof under its control, in accomplishing its vast schemes of ambition and war. And in its fully-developed form, Russia will probably constitute the great Gog of scripture—Gog the prince of *Rosh* of Meshech and Tubal, who is described by Ezekiel, and who will be destroyed in the great battle of Armageddon as predicted. The present aspect of things in Europe looks suspiciously in this direction. But whatever may be true in respect to these things, there can be no doubt that, according to prophecy, we are on the eve of vast political revolutions, in which probably blood will flow as described in apocalyptic vision. But these things, as they come to pass, will only hasten on the day of deliverance and salvation.

9. The very general expectation upon the minds of most persons, that we are approaching some great crisis, is an indication of the coming Saviour.

Forthcoming events cast their shadows before them. So do these shadow forth the near approach of the Son of Man, and our children may see the day if we do not. May God hasten it, in its time. It is our hope and joy. *Amen.*

Chapter Ninth.

THE FACT, NATURE, AND RATIONALITY OF THE RESURRECTION OF OUR MATERIAL BODIES.

THE following discourse does not form an essential part of the argument, contained in the preceding chapters, and might therefore be left out without injuring its proportions. But, as much is said in them respecting the resurrection of the dead, and as, in the minds of many, there is much doubt and perplexity in regard to the resurrection; it has been thought that it might be useful, and serve more clearly to illustrate the themes already discussed to insert it.

It is manifest from the teachings and writings of the apostles of our Lord, that the doctrine of the resurrection of the dead was in their estimation fundamental to the whole Christian system, and to all the hopes inspired by the gospel.

The apostle Paul says, 1 Cor. 15: 12–17.—"Now if Christ be preached that he rose from the dead, how say some among you that there is no resurrection of the dead? But if there be no resurrection of the dead, then is Christ not risen. And if Christ be not risen, then is our preaching vain, and your faith is also vain. Yea, and we are found false witnesses of God; because we have testified of God that he raised up Christ: whom he raised not up, if so be that the dead rise not. For if the dead rise not, then is not Christ raised; and if Christ be not raised, your faith is vain; ye are yet in your sins."

No language could more strongly declare the essential importance of this doctrine to the Christian system than this, and its intimate and necessary connection with all our immortal hopes. And hence the apostles, wherever they went, bore witness to the reality of the resurrection of Christ from the dead, as the crowning miracle in the chain of evidence submitted in proof of the gospel, and as a sure pledge of all that God had promised of a blissful immortality in the world to come.

It is then a matter of infinite moment to all who have fled for refuge, to lay hold on the hope set before them in the gospel, to hold fast the resurrection of our material bodies from the dead, and to understand all that Heaven has been pleased to reveal respecting its nature and glory.

In presenting this subject it is proposed to prove the fact of the resurrection of our material bodies, and to illustrate the Bible doctrine respecting it; and

2. To show that it is in harmony with reason, with our immortal and aspiring natures, with all the works of Jehovah, and opens before the believer a career of immortality inconceivably grand and glorious.

1. The Bible teaches that it is that which dies which is to be raised from the dead, and consequently it teaches that the resurrection from the dead is the reconstruction and reanimation of our material bodies.

Some who deny the resurrection of the body, say that the resurrection is only the elimination, or the rising of the spiritual part of man from the body at death. This we believe, is the doctrine of Swedenborg. But this is no resurrection of the dead, and is clearly not the doctrine of scripture. Nothing could be taught more definitely by human language, than is the fact that it is that part of man which dies, which is to be raised up. In proof of this we present—

1. The resurrection of our Lord Jesus Christ. In many scriptures it is explicitly declared that the crucified Jesus did rise from the dead. But in what did his resurrection

consist? Unquestionably in the reanimation of that body which died—which was taken down from the cross, and laid in the sepulchre of Joseph of Arimathea. Of this there is the most positive and abundant proof.

In the second chapter of John's gospel we are told, that on a certain occasion, when the Jews demanded of our Lord a sign in testimony of his authority for doing what he did, He said, "Destroy this temple, and in three days I will raise it up." The Jews misunderstanding his reference, said, "Forty and six years was this temple"—the temple at Jerusalem—"in building, and wilt thou rear it up in three days?" But he spake of the temple of his body. When, therefore, he was risen from the dead, his disciples remembered that he had said this unto them; and they believed the scripture and the word which Jesus had said."

In this passage the question is put beyond all rational controversy, that the Saviour, in predicting his own resurrection on the third day, had respect to his material body; for it was that which the Jews could and would destroy that was to be raised up. But the spiritual nature of Christ they could not touch or destroy, and hence it was clearly not his spiritual body which was predicted to rise, but his mortal, material body. And all this is fully illustrated and confirmed in the events that followed.

When our Lord said to the Jews, Destroy this temple—this body of mine, and in three days I will raise it up, He fully committed himself on a point from which there was no retreat, and in regard to which there was no room for evasion. The truth of his claims, as the Messiah, was fully and deliberately staked upon this single fact, that if they put him to death, as he knew they meditated, he would rise again to life in that same body on the third day. If he arose, then, agreeably to his own prediction, it would demonstrate his pretensions; if not, the failure would prove him an impostor.

This point, those who were instrumental in his death well understood, and they determined to put his claims here to the most rigid scrutiny. And hence we find this record—Matt. 27 : 6–2 : "Now the next day that followed the day of the preparation, the chief priests and Pharisees came together unto Pilate, saying, Sir, we remember that that deceiver said, while he was yet alive, *After three days I will rise again.* Command, therefore, that the sepulchre be made sure until the third day, lest his disciples come by night, and steal him away, and say unto the people, He is risen from the dead: so the last error shall be worse than the first."

Now all this arrangement could have reference only to that body which had died, and it showed a determination to test the truth or falsehood of the Saviour's pretensions to the utmost, confident of a triumph over him whom they regarded with abhorence.

When the dead body of our Lord was therefore laid in the tomb, and the stone which closed the door sealed—around that sepulchre the most wakeful suspicion prevailed, the most watchful vigilance was exercised, and every precaution was taken to guard that body, in order to decide the fact whether that body which died, and was laid in the grave, should continue there lifeless beyond the specified time, or rise to life again as predicted.

It was a time of deep anxiety and suspense. The powers of light and darkness all around were awake and watching the result. The soldiers silently paraded about the tomb, and the chief priests and Pharisees anticipating a triumph, awaited the issue with deep and anxious emotion.

Hour after hour rolled away. The first and the second nights were passed and all was still. But the third day came, and that temple which had been destroyed was rebuilt—that body which was laid in the tomb was reanimated, and reunited to that immortal part which went with the soul of the penitent thief to paradise on the day of his death.

Of this there is the most ample proof in the several accounts given by the evangelists, appointed as witnesses of his resurrection.

Passing over many incontrovertible circumstances which demonstrate the resurrection of *that material body* of our Lord which was crucified and died, we will first notice his appearance to his disciples at Jerusalem, recorded in Luke 24: 36–46. He had appeared to two of the brethren on their way to Emmaus, and was made known to them in the breaking of bread. While these two were relating to the eleven what things were done in the way, and how he was made known to them, Jesus himself suddenly stood in the midst of them, and said, "Peace be unto you. But they were terrified and affrighted, and supposed that they had seen a spirit. And he said unto them, Why are ye terrified? and why do thoughts arise in your hearts? Behold my hands and my feet, that it is I myself; handle me and see; for a spirit hath not flesh and bones as ye see me have. And when he had thus spoken, he showed them his hands and his feet, bearing the marks of the nails. And while they yet believed not for joy, and wondered, he said unto them, Have ye here any meat? And they gave him a piece of a broiled fish and of a honey-comb. And he took it and did eat it before them."

This is an exceedingly interesting passage, and one which demonstrates, by a series of facts, the reality of the resurrection of the material body of our Lord. The disciples affrighted, supposed it was a spirit they saw; but to correct this impression, the risen Saviour exhorted them not to be troubled, but to come and satisfy themselves that he was not a spirit, by beholding his hands and his feet—the very scars of the wounds which had been made by the piercing of the nails and the spear: showing that it was the same body that was crucified, that had been raised, and in no sense a merely spiritual, ethereal, or sublimated substance.

2. The Saviour positively declared that he was not a spirit, but had a body with flesh and bones as other men. "Behold my hands and my feet, that it is I myself: handle me and see, for a spirit hath not flesh and bones as ye see me have." He shows us here, a distinction between body and spirit. A spirit hath not flesh and bones. It is something distinct from matter. But he, in his resurrection body, had flesh and bones, and therefore manifestly had a material body.

3. And then, further to demonstrate to them this great fact, which he seemed anxious to impress upon them, that he was not as pirit, but had a material body, He said, "Have ye here any meat? And they gave him a piece of a broiled fish, and a honey-comb, and he took it and did eat it before them." Now the Lord did, in truth, eat this fish and honey-comb, or he did not. If he did not, he was guilty of practicing upon them a gross deception. If he did eat them, it demonstrates that he had a material body as really as before his crucifixion.

It is then certain, from this scripture, as well as from other parallel passages, which he who doubts should consult, that it was that part of our Lord which died, which rose again. And this proves that the scriptural doctrine of the resurrection is, that it is that which dies, which is raised, or is to be raised; for, says the apostle, "Now is Christ risen from the dead, and become the first fruits of them that sleep." His resurrection is a proof and pledge, and an illustration of that of others, which could not be, were his not of the same nature and character as all others.

In determining, therefore, that the resurrection body of

our Lord was a material body, we have decided the question, that our resurrection bodies will also be material. For we are definitely informed by the apostle, in his Epistle to the Philippians, 3 : 21, "That when the Lord comes, he will change our vile bodies that they may be fashioned like unto his glorious body, according to the working of his mighty power, whereby he is able to subdue all things unto himself."

In this passage the pattern is given according to which our bodies are to be formed in the resurrection; so that whatever was the nature of the resurrection body of our Lord, such will undoubtedly be ours. But it has been shown that he rose in his material body—in a body that could be handled—that bore in it the prints of the nails and the spear, and which could eat and drink; and it is therefore demonstrated from scripture, that the resurrection of all others will be material.

This is still further confirmed by the express teachings of our Lord, in John 5 : 25–28. In asserting his high authority and power in this most interesting passage, Christ says, "Verily, verily, I say unto you, the hour is coming, and now is, when the dead shall hear the voice of the Son of God: and they that hear shall live." Now mark, it is that which is dead, not the living spirit, which is to hear the voice of the Son of God and live. From the fact that our Lord says, that the hour is not only coming, *but now is*, when the dead shall hear his voice, some have argued that only a spiritual resurrection was here intended. But there is no ground or necessity in the passage for any such conclusion. Was it not a fact, that at that hour or time, the dead did hear the voice of the Son of God and live? Did he not frequently, during his ministry, raise the dead to life? Did not Lazarus, and the son of the lone widow of Nain, and the daughter of Jairus, and many others who were dead, hear the voice of the Son of God miraculously put forth, and live? Our Lord, therefore, in affirming that the dead at that time heard his voice, was only declaring what was everywhere, in Judea, known to be the fact. And to show his power to do all that he had said respecting the resurrection of the dead universally, he refers to these facts which were at that time repeatedly occurring, in answer to the voice of the Son of God.

But he goes on to say; "Marvel not at this: for the hour is coming in which all that are *in their graves* shall hear his voice, and shall come forth; they that have done good unto the resurrection of life; and they that have done evil unto the resurrection of damnation." It is here clearly predicted that those who are to hear the voice of the Son of God, are those who are in their graves. But the bodies only of the dead are in the grave—therefore the resurrection of the material body is certainly taught. The scriptural testimony in favor of the resurrection of our material bodies, is so abundant, that it would be impossible to consider it in one short discourse.

The resurrection of our material bodies from the grave, is undoubtedly purely a scriptural doctrine, and must depend entirely on its testimony. And yet in the light which the Scriptures shed upon this subject, a presumptive argument may be drawn in its favor from the wonderful mechanism and powers of the human body. The mechanism of the human frame is exceedingly curious, and intricately wonderful. The body is a temple or dwelling place of the immortal mind, and was designed as a combination of instruments through which its development and external manifestation was to be made to the world, and its divinely derived powers exercised and exhibited. Now, the wonderful powers of the human body, and its wisely and nicely-adjusted adaptation to the faculties and destiny of the mind, seem clearly to indicate that its existence will be necessary to the full development of mind in a future world, and to its highest welfare.

1. Consider what astonishing and wonderful powers the members of the body possess, as instruments of the soul, as manifested in all the beautiful, the useful, the noble and grand productions of mechanical art, as seen in the world. Who rears the beautiful mansion, the gorgeous temple, and adorns them with all their splendid and architectural members and proportions? Who forms and puts together the complicated, the highly-finished, and nicely-adjusted parts of a steam engine, and other machinery by which the elements of nature are appropriated to the use of man, and by which the most beautiful and astonishing results are produced? By what agency has the magnetic telegraph been constructed, by which the lightning is made to answer to the call of man, and to furnish a highway of thought for the nations? The answer is, by the instrumentalities of the members of the human body. The mind conceived and devised these combinations of wisdom, utility and beauty, but the mind could never have executed its conceptions, or have given form to its ideas in external nature and development, had it not been for its mechanical agent, the body, furnished for its use by the Great Creator.

In every triumph of mechanical art, we see not only the manifestations of active intellect, but the wonderful powers and adaptations of the human body to all the conceptions and combinations of the ever-active and aspiring mind. It is manifest that the body is now necessary to the development and highest achievements of mind, and essential to its welfare and happiness. Will it not be so hereafter? Will not the mind need a body, with powers similar to those now possessed, refined and augmented, as its minister or agent in the execution of those wonderful schemes which will be devised and enjoyed in its enlarged and eternal development? Will the mind, in a future world, be able to do its will, and accomplish its pleasure independently of a body as now possessed, and better attain the high destinies of its being? Certainly we are not warranted in such a conclusion by any thing we can see within or about us in the present world.

The body, with its various mechanical organs and powers, is now essential to the mind. What could the spirit do without it? What execute of good or evil? Now, the fact that the body is so essential to the operations of mind in the present world, seems clearly to intimate that a body must be essential to its highest well-being in any world. And this truth the Scriptures declare in the doctrine of the resurrection; and hence it may be seen that the doctrine is rational, and in accordance with the nature and wants of the mind.

But if the mind, as some suppose, will rise to a higher state of perfection when emancipated from the body—if it will then be free from all that impedes and clogs its upward progress, why was it ever connected with the body? Is it not an impeachment, virtually, of the wisdom and goodness of the Creator, to say that the body is a clog to the mind, and that it will better attain its highest end when disconnected with matter? We repeat the inquiry, Why, according to this supposition, did God form for man a material body, with such wonderful mechanical powers, and associate it essentially with the mind in all its present pursuits, probation and enjoyments? Did he do it that he might simply dash it to pieces at death, as a vile vessel? Or only that in it, he might imprison and impede, afflict and torment the spirit? How unreasonable!

In many cases the association of mind with the body in this life answers no valuable purpose. How many die in infancy and childhood! How many by bodily diseases and deformity only suffer! Did God make these in vain? Now, there is no way in which we can conceive that the wisdom and goodness of God can be vindicated, in the construction of the human form, and its essential association with mind, but on the ground of the scriptural doctrine—that he intended the body to be as immortal as the mind and its eternal associate and helper. Had man never sinned, according to scripture, his body would have lived on in immortal bloom, as long as his mind.

But sin for a time has interrupted the order of Heaven, and death has entered our world. But the second Adam will restore the ruins of the first, and reëstablish the union of mind with matter, in an ever-endeared, immortal, and glorious form.

But there are other and higher powers of the human body than these which have been named; which also seem clearly to intimate its high and glorious destiny. How wonderful, for example, are the powers of eloquence! What vast multitudes have been charmed, and enchanted, and swayed to and fro as the trees of the forest before the tempest by the eloquence of such men as Demosthenes and Cicero in ancient times, and in modern times, by such men as Whitefield and a Patrick Henry! And yet there have been multitudes in the world equally as eminent in their sphere as these.

Now all this power of eloquence is not merely the effect of mind: for could the mind be thus eloquent, and produce these thrilling effects independently of the body? Surely not. To produce the result, the lungs heave, the muscles of the throat contract and dilate—the tongue moves obedient to the will—the lips open or are compressed—the countenance beams, and the eye lightens and sparkles with emotion, and the whole body moves and gestures the sentiments and passions of the soul. Could the mind then be eloquent without the body?

Now all these things go to show the wonderful powers of the body, and its perfect adaptation to the nature, and desires, and designs of the presiding spirit. Can the mind do without these aids and powers in another life? Who that was authorized has ever said that it can?

And then, too, see the power of music performed through material organs, to charm and elevate and enrapture the soul. It would seem that God has raised up a Jenny Lind for the purpose of showing what the human voice can do, and what it may become under favorable circumstances. What thousands hang in ecstacy upon the thrilling notes which warble from her throat! How strangely wonderful that organism which can produce these exciting and pleasing effects! And yet, no doubt, there are thousands equally gifted in the wide world, unknown and uncultivated; for,

> "Full many a gem of purest ray serene,
> The dark, unfathomed caves of ocean bear;
> Full many a flower is born to blush unseen,
> And waste its sweetness on the desert air."

Will their sweetness never be known? Is there not another life where their fragrance will be exhaled, producing delighted emotions? Now, if such thrilling effects can be produced by music on earth, performed through material organs, oh, what will be the music of that great multitude, which no man can number, around the throne, whose voices in the resurrection state will, as now, be the result of material organization, tuned to sweetest harmony and love, as it comes over the soul as the rushing of mighty waters, or as the whispers of the gentlest zephyrs! Can it be that this bodily organism, capable of such wonderful effects, is only destined to live during life's short years of suffering and trial? Or does not rather nature intimate that a body so marvelous in its construction, and so wisely adapted to the uses and desires of the mind, should live and accompany the immortal spirit in all its eternal progress?

All these considerations serve to show the entire harmony

of the doctrine of the resurrection of our material bodies, as taught in scripture, with the nature of the human soul, and its highest development and welfare. And this harmony and adaptation might be further argued from the exquisite arrangement and power of the nervous system to communicate the most intense pleasure to the soul, as is often seen, and from the activities of all the senses in bringing the mind into intimate communication with the perfections of God, manifested in the boundless material creation.

To the resurrection of our material bodies there are some objections constantly urged by the unbelieving, which it will be important to consider, before we proceed to consider more extendedly the glorious and immortal results of the doctrine.

1. Our bodies die, and are in the course of dissolution resolved into their original elements. Often the substances of which they are composed are scattered, and borne in particles and fragments to widely different parts of the earth; and in the processes of nature enter again and again into the composition of vegetables and animal bodies indefinitely. Now, from this, unbelievers have maintained that it is an utter impossibility and an absurdity, that the dead should be raised, whose bodies have been dissolved, dissipated and formed into countless new combinations. But this objection rests upon a false assumption in regard to what is necessary to constitute personal identity, and a perverted view of the teachings of scripture. It supposes that all, and the very same particles of matter which compose our bodies when they die, or before death, must necessarily be gathered from their wide dispersion throughout the world, and extracted from every other combination, vegetable, animal, or human, into which they may have entered and reconstructed, if the dead are ever raised. But as some of the substances which compose the body of one man, when he dies, may have en-

tered into the body of another when he died, the resurrection of the self-same body is regarded as utterly impossible.

But the scriptures do not teach that the same particles of matter in all respects will enter into our future bodies, or be at all necessary to the resurrection. When they declare that the dead will be raised, they use the language of common life, and mean that our raised bodies will be the bodies that died, in the same sense that our bodies are the same at different periods of our lives. When it is said that a man has the same body now that he had twenty years ago, nothing absurd or that is contrary to consciousness is uttered. Every one feels and believes that he has at all times the same body in a popular sense, however great the changes produced by waste and supply. It bears every scar, or mark, or deformity once made permanently upon it. And yet it is well known that, philosophically speaking, a man has not a body composed of the same particles of matter at any two distinct periods of his life. But yet a full knowledge of this does not alter his consciousness that he is always the same being in soul and body.

At one period of a man's life, he is in the bloom of health, and then in a short time he is reduced by disease to a mere skeleton, and then again the return of health clothes him with new flesh and vigor. And yet through all these changes, he feels and knows that he has the same body, as a matter of consciousness, and in accordance with the language of common life.

It is supposed that our bodies by waste and accretion undergo an entire change once in seven years. And yet have I not the same body I had seven years ago? I feel that I am myself, and recognize my body as the same. Now the sum of all this is, that the same identical particles of matter or substances, are not necessary at all times to constitute personal identity. Any human form may throw off by piece-meal, the whole of the matter contained in its formation, and take to itself new substances of the same kind, and according to the same laws of organization, and still preserve its conscious identity. All this we know to be true.

So in the resurrection, it will not be necessary that all the same substances should enter into the raised bodies, which were in them at death, to constitute them the same. This the scriptures abundantly declare, and they are thus in harmony with constantly observed facts in physiology. In 1 Cor. 15, the apostle Paul teaches most definitely that our resurrection bodies will not be composed of all the same particles of matter as in life.

In answer to the question, "How are the dead raised up, and with what bodies do they come?" He says, "Thou fool, that which thou sowest is not quickened except it die: and that which thou sowest, thou sowest not that body which shall be, but it bears grain; it may chance of wheat or some other grain. But God giveth it a body as it hath pleased him, and to every seed his own," or its own body; that is, he gives to wheat the body of wheat, to corn the body of corn, and so on from whatever kind of seed is sown there springs a like body.

The apostle does not intend to say that there is a perfect analogy between grain sown and human bodies buried in the grave; but he does mean to teach, that as from grain sown, and which dies in the ground, there springs another body or grain of the same kind, though not containing the same particles of matter: so from our dead bodies buried in earth, there will at the resurrection spring another body of the same kind, and containing perhaps enough of the old body to render the new one the same. "It is, perhaps, a twentieth part of a grain of wheat which is sown and dies in the ground, which springs up and forms a part of the new grain;

the rest rots in the ground and remains. It is not needed in the new body which God gives the wheat, and is not called forth again. So we are taught, our bodies which die will not be the same as to particles of matter as those which rise." Old particles will be dropped, and for ought we know, new ones assumed, in that wonderful change which is to fit us for the high destinies in reserve.

If, then, all the same particles of matter which constitute our present bodies, do not, or will not enter into our future bodies, the argument against the resurrection founded upon the assumption that they will, and that they cannot be gathered up, entirely fails; for they are not necessary to accomplish all that the Scriptures predict.

Admitting, then, that large portions of the human body after death do enter into the composition of other living bodies, so that it would be impossible to gather them up to reincorporate them in the new ones, the whole difficulty vanishes at once on the scriptural doctrine that all the same particles will not be raised. As God can give to the wheat a new body, and yet it be wheat still possessing the same nature; so he can in the resurrection, if need be, give new bodies, and yet preserve our personal identity.

The scriptures teach that our resurrection bodies will not only not contain all the matter they now do, but that, in many respects, they will be very different from what they now are, and far more beautiful and glorious. They will pass through a wonderful change or transformation, in their resurrection and transition to immortal glory. This wonderful transformation is clearly and beautifully intimated in the apostle's description. He says of the body, "It is sown in corruption, it is raised in incorruption: it is sown in dishonor, it is raised in glory: it is sown in weakness, it is raised in power: it is sown a natural body, it is raised a spiritual body." And again, he says, "Behold, I show you a mystery: we shall not all sleep, but we shall all be changed, in a moment, in the twinkling of an eye, at the last trump; for the trumpet shall sound and the dead shall be raised incorruptible, and we shall be changed. For this corruptible must put on incorruption, and this mortal must put on immortality."

This language certainly denotes a most wonderful and glorious change in the raised bodies, yet not such as to destroy our conscious and acknowledged identity.

1. It is sown in corruption. All the tendencies of the body at death are to loathsome corruption and dissolution. In life, we are subject to disease and decay, and our dead we are compelled to bury out of our sight. But it will be raised in incorruption. It will then be so changed that it will be no longer subject to disease, decay and death.

2. It is sown in dishonor. It is laid in the grave an unsightly object, and it dies as a malefactor under the righteous sentence of Heaven. But in the resurrection it will be exceedingly beautiful. It will be raised in glory. It will be fashioned like unto Christ's body, and made resplendent with his beauty. As God forms the diamond so beautiful from charcoal, the blackest of substances, so he will of the corruptible and inglorious body, form one in the resurrection surpassingly beautiful, and resplendently glorious.

3. It is sown in weakness. And how exceedingly weak it is! How incapable of resisting the attacks of disease, or the thousand agents at work for its destruction! How the strong man bows and sinks a helpless thing into the embraces of the tomb! Surely it is sown in weakness; but it will be raised in power. In the raised state, it will, no doubt, be endowed with wonderful powers—with the power of resisting all evil—with vastly-increased powers of locomotion—with powers fully adequate to all the wants and energies, and pure desires of the aspiring mind. It will know fatigue no more,

nor exhaustion, and will not need to be invigorated by sleep and tender care as now.

4. It is sown a natural body. It is now a body possessed of many merely animal instincts and sensual propensities and appetites. It hungers and thirsts, and is subject to many vile affections by which the mind is often degraded and enslaved. But not so in the resurrection. It will be raised a spiritual body—that is, a body freed from all merely animal and degrading propensities. It will be a body entirely and perfectly adapted to the wants and pursuits of the mind which is spiritual, and entirely under its control. It will hence be a spiritual body—a body entirely adapted to, and subservient to spirit, and no longer under the dominion of the flesh. Hence we are assured by the Saviour, that in the resurrection we shall neither marry nor be given in marriage, but shall be all as the angels of God, and equal one to another.

From the fact, that in the resurrection our bodies are to be spiritual, some have argued that they would no longer be material. But this cannot be true; for it has already been shown that it must and will be material. The term spiritual here is not used in opposition to that which is material, but to that which is merely natural or animal. The phraseology of the passage shows conclusively that this spiritual body is material still; for, let it be noticed, it is the corruptible body that is changed into the incorruptible the loathsome dishonored body which becomes the beautiful, and glorious, the weak that is changed into the powerful, and the natural body we now have, which rises to the spiritual; for, says the apostle, we must all be changed. Now, is there any evidence that God ever does, or can, change matter into spirit?

The fact that it is this corruptible, natural body, which we now have, that is changed into the spiritual, shows that the spiritual body cannot be spirit. It is a body denominated spiritual, we judge, because it will be adapted, in a high degree, to spirit. Freed from all merely animal and groveling propensities, it will become subservient preëminently and only to the higher destinies of the immortal mind. It will be material still after its transformation, only in a state of higher perfection than we now possess. The resurrection body of our Lord was no doubt spiritual, and yet we have seen that it was material, having the distinctive properties of matter, and bearing about in it the infallible marks that it was the same that was crucified. And the scriptures give us no intimation that his body was changed from matter to spirit, at his ascension. Now, as our *vile bodies* are to be changed, and fashioned like unto his glorious body, it is certain that they must be material. A body entirely subservient to mind, and the minister and executor only of its holy and benevolent purposes, may with great propriety be called a spiritual body. And such may be the control of the spirit over the body in the resurrection state, that it may transport it, at will, from place to place, or from world to world, as our Lord seemed to have conveyed his, without the usual slow process of locomotion.

Again, the apostle assures us, 1 Cor. 15, "That flesh and blood cannot inherit the kingdom of God." From this, some have supposed that material bodies, such as the Saviour had after his resurrection, cannot enter heaven. But there are many forms and modifications of matter which are not flesh and blood, and therefore the declaration that flesh and blood as they are now constituted, unchanged, and unpurified, cannot inherit the kingdom of God, does not assert that material bodies, in some form, may not enter. Let these vile bodies be so changed that they shall no longer be flesh and blood as they now are, and the declaration of our Lord would no longer apply.

But the connection in which these words are found, and

the qualifying and explanatory exposition given, shows what the apostle meant, and that he had no idea of teaching that our bodies would not be material as much so as they now are.

He says, "Now this I say, brethren, that flesh and blood cannot inherit the kingdom of God; neither doth corruption inherit incorruption. Behold, I show you a mystery: We shall not all sleep (or die,) but we shall *all* be changed, in a moment, in the twinkling of an eye, at the last trump: for the trumpet shall sound, and the dead shall be raised incorruptible, *and we shall be changed.* For this corruption must put on incorruption, and this mortal must put on immortality. So when this corruption shall have put on incorruption, and this mortal shall have put on immortality, then shall be brought to pass the saying that is written, Death is swallowed up in victory. O death, where is thy sting? O grave, where is thy victory? The sting of death is sin; and the strength of sin is the law; But thanks be to God, which giveth us the victory, through our Lord Jesus Christ."

Now, is it not manifest from this description of the apostle, that he did not contemplate the dropping or laying aside of the material body, *but only its change* from mortal to immortal, from corruption to incorruption. He meant to say that flesh and blood as now constituted, or the human body in its present gross, mortal, and corruptible state, could not partake of the pure and refined pleasures of an immortal, incorruptible state. To fit it for these, it must undergo a change in order to adapt it to its higher and more glorious sphere of being and enjoyment. It is manifest that the apostle meant nothing more than this; for he says "that when *this corruptible* shall have put on incorruption, and *this mortal* shall have put on immortality, *then* shall be brought to pass the saying that is written, *Death is swallowed up* in victory. O death, where is thy sting? O grave, where is thy victory?" Now. if it is not the material body that is raised, then there is no triumph over death or the grave. Death holds all he ever gets, and the grave continues to sway his cruel sceptre over the generations of the dead forever. This exulting and triumphant language can have force only in application of the resurrection of the material body which dies. In its resurrection, a change will be produced in it miraculously, by the power of God, to fit it for a higher sphere; but it will be material still, and may have *flesh and bones,* as the Saviour had after his resurrection, if it has not *flesh and blood* in its present corruptible and mortal constitution.

We have in nature many emblems of the transformation of our mortal bodies, which strikingly and beautifully illustrate the changes through which a body may pass in fitting it for a higher sphere of being, without changing its material nature, or destroying its identity. Innumerable worms, and the loathsome caterpillar, which we would, perhaps, shudder to touch, creeping beneath our feet, are transformed from the larva to the beautiful chrysalis, and thence to the gaudy butterfly; whence it rises to a new sphere of life, subsistence, and enjoyment, winging its way on downy wings over smiling nature, and sipping at every flower which God has opened for its pleasure. Now, that worm is just as much material in its higher state of development, as in its lower, and were it endowed with memory and intelligence, it would, perhaps, feel conscious that it was the same identical being through all its changes.

So, in the resurrection, we may pass through just as great a change, as does the caterpillar, and still preserve our materiality and conscious identity. In that change from mortal to immortal, from corruption to incorruption, from weakness to power, which is to fit us for our higher sphere of being, our bodies may be as much more beautiful than they are now, as the butterfly is than the caterpillar, and our powers of locomotion and sphere of enjoyment may as greatly transcend those now possessed, as do those of the soaring butterfly, the crawling worm. What is there, then, unnatural, unreasonable, or undesirable in the resurrection of our material bodies?

But without dwelling longer on the proof of the resurrection of our material bodies, or its illustration, we will proceed to consider briefly, some of the glorious consequences and manifold results of the resurrection. And—

1. One of the most obvious consequences of the resurrection of our material bodies, will be, that we shall be forever connected with the material universe—with all these wonderful works of God, unlimitable, and unsearchable, which exist in the world, and in the universe around us: and this, too, under circumstances most favorable for investigation, improvement, and boundless enjoyment. Our bodies will be material bodies, rendered immortal, incorruptible, perfect, beautiful, and glorious, with all the senses complete and perfect, and in full exercise, and all under the control of a holy mind.

Our minds are now too generally the servants of the body. Too often, all their noble faculties and powers are enslaved by a degrading sensuality, or by the necessary wants and craving of our now mortal and weak natures.

But in the resurrection it will not be so. It is easy to conceive of the reverse of all this, when every sense, and faculty, and power of the body shall become wholly subservient to the highest intellectual and moral enjoyment; when the eye shall not only bring to our knowledge and enjoyment everything that is beautiful in the glorious universe, but be employed as an instrument in making observations upon God's wondrous works, from those mighty orbs which roll unnumbered around us, down to the smallest insect; and from the mysterious laws which bind suns and planets into harmonious systems and motions, down to the hidden principles which govern universal nature in all its productions.

Then the ear shall not only listen with enraptured emotion to the melody and harmony of sweet sounds, and exulting music as it bursts from the swelling anthems of the redeemed, but shall be a means of social intercourse, of the reception of knowledge and enjoyment, and endless improvement.

Then the tongue, no longer an unruly member, full of deadly poison, shall be the means of conveying to others the pure sentiments of the soul, the knowledge we have acquired, and the discoveries we have made, as well as an instrument by which we shall join in the music of heaven and speak forth the praises of Jehovah. And so all other senses developed or undeveloped, under the control of a holy mind, and in connection with the material universe, may be employed in the highest pursuits and purest enjoyments.

All this flows necessarily as a consequence from the nature of our resurrection. And it is easy to see that the scriptural view of the resurrection of our material bodies, placing us thus in connection with the material universe, under the most favorable and exalted circumstances, gives to our future existence a reality and a substantiality which no other view can, and opens before the mind visions of glory inconceivably grand and magnificent. It does not separate us from matter, and all the loved forms and objects of the material universe, as do all merely spiritual theories, and place us in communication with a world of ghosts, of phantasies and phantasms; but it brings us in connection, and identifies us with God's glorious universe, the delighted spectators of his mighty works, and the students of his vast and now incomprehensible designs.

This leads to another remark and consequence of the resurrection, which is, that our knowledge of God, and of his attributes, will be acquired in a future state as now, for the most part, through the works of his hands.

It is manifest that we now have no knowledge of God,

which was not derived primarily through the medium of sensation, from our contact and intercourse with the material world. Whatever God has been pleased to reveal of himself in his Word, has a direct reference to his works, or to the objects and operations of nature by and through which his incomprehensible perfections are exhibited. And when he would reveal to us more clearly his moral character, and commend to us more attractively his love, he did it not simply by abstract announcement, but by manifesting himself in the flesh, and thus seeking through the medium of a material body to illustrate himself to his creatures.

Is it not true, therefore, that the clearest, brightest views we have of God, or that creatures have ever enjoyed, are those of God manifest in the flesh? And how tender, affecting, and soul-cheering, is the knowledge and condescension here communicated! In what other way could the Infinite and the Invisible so clearly and becomingly have made himself known? It seems, therefore, certain that all correct knowledge of God and his attributes is now derived, in some form, from his works, or through material form, and all our ideas of him are materialized, being clothed in drapery drawn from the external world. Will this be so hereafter? It will, according to the doctrine of the resurrection. In all our employments, investigations, and enjoyments in a future world, we shall be constantly concerned with material objects, as well as conversant with spiritual beings. There will then exist a most striking resemblance between our present and our future existence. The one will be but the continuation of the other, in a higher and purer state than any earthly mind has ever conceived. Nor is there anything unreasonable in all this. It is all in entire harmony with the nature and capacities of the mind, and with the works of God in their adaptation to the mind through a material body. And it is highly probable, if not certain, that our bodies will be as necessary to the full development and action of the mind in a future life, as here. To accomplish all that God has designed in our creation, we shall need the agency of all our senses and bodily members as now, or God would never raise the dead, as it is predicted he will. The doctrine of the resurrection, then, is in entire harmony with all that we can now see or know, and with our immortal aspirings.

And what a field for seeing, for thought, and enjoyment, will God's boundless universe open to us in the resurrection state. Suppose our bodies were now free from all disease, infirmity, or imperfection, and rendered incapable of corruption, pain, weakness, or fatigue, and were endowed with the power of ascending, by the will of God, to any world, to see the wonders of Godhead there displayed, or to speed our way on some mission of love to some distant orb, would not this be a glorious prospect? And with a God to minister to our wants, and to direct our career, what higher perfection or felicity could we desire? Such is the resurrection state, and such its glorious consequence.

Another consequence of the resurrection of our material bodies, will be, that our bodies which have been associated with us in all our trials, and conflicts, and sufferings in life, will share with us in all the rewards of the world to come; and all the dear forms which we have here loved, rendered glorious and immortal, will still be embraced in bonds of sweetest friendship and love.

All this would seem to be only a matter of justice. Through life, the body has been the companion of the mind, and has been associated with it in all its probation, and in all its pursuits of righteousness or unrighteousness, in training it for the destiny for which it is fitted. And is it not right that it should share with it in that destiny? Does not justice seem to demand that the two which have been united on earth should be indissolubly united in the world to come, and mutual sharers in its destinies?

The beings, then, that shall inhabit the future world will be no mere ghosts or spirits, whom no one can touch or embrace. Theirs will be no mere shadowy, gauzy existence, but a tangible, and bodily reality. There will be the warm embrace of friendship, and the real song of praise performed through material organs, giving utterance to the ardent devotions of sinless souls. Eye will sparkle to eye, and heart will beat to heart, and hand will be joined in hand, amid the assemblies and communings of the just in that better land and purer state.

The doctrine of the resurrection, as presented in scripture, is strikingly in harmony with the views advocated in the preceding chapters.

It is in entire harmony, as we have seen, with the perpetuity of the earth, and the material universe through eternal ages; for, if our material bodies are to be raised and glorified, then clearly there must exist, also, a material universe with which they shall be associated.

The doctrine also shows how it is that the raised saints may hold intercourse with the unglorified on earth, and reign over them as ministering agents, without involving any absurdity.

The idea which some entertain, that it would be inappropriate for the raised and transfigured saints, to dwell in a material world, finds no resting-place according to these views. And such an idea is manifestly unscriptural. Heaven is, no doubt, a place which has a distinct locality, and so are the mansions in our Father's house, which Jesus has gone to prepare. And if they are places, they must be material places; for, can a place be made of spirit?

Reader! ponder these things, and if you search the scriptures, you will find that with the resurrection are associated all for which God, in his word, has authorized you to hope, and all that he has promised to give. The resurrection should be a prominent theme of discourse, and a never failing source of consolation to the pious. "For our conversation is in heaven, from whence also we look for the Saviour, the Lord Jesus Christ: Who shall change our *vile body*, that it may be fashioned like unto his glorious body, according to the working whereby he is able even to subdue all things unto himself."—Phil. 3: 20, 21.

www.ingramcontent.com/pod-product-compliance
Lightning Source LLC
LaVergne TN
LVHW010253110826
845151LV00004B/1466

* 9 7 8 1 4 2 5 5 2 2 4 2 1 *